P9-DCO-664

Raising the Roof

The Pastoral-to-Program Size Transition

Alice Mann

AN ALBAN INSTITUTE PUBLICATION

Scriptural quotations, unless otherwise noted, are from the New Revised Standard Version of the Bible, copyright © 2001, Division of Christian Education of the National Council of the Churches of Christ in the United States of America, and are used by permission.

Copyright © 2001 by the Alban Institute. All rights reserved.

This material may not be photocopied or reproduced in any way without written permission. Go to http://www.alban.org/permissions.asp

Library of Congress Catalog Card Number 2001094868

ISBN 1-56699-254-0

10   09   08   07   06   05   WP   5   6   7   8   9   10   11

CONTENTS

FIGURES

[Handwritten note at top of page:]

Context - a putting together - to weave together
The parts of a sentence paragraph, because its
immediately next to or surrounding a specified
word or passage and determining its exact
meaning. to quote a remark out of context
② The whole situation, back ground, environment
relevant to a particular event, personality,
creation its

In times of size transition, congregations have an opportunity to deepen the connection between faith and context. Vital congregations are passionate about bringing faith to bear powerfully within their context—I believe this right down to my toes.

FAITH MEETING CONTEXT

If you look carefully at the founding story of your own church, you will almost certainly find that its early life—including prayer, belief, action in the world—was shaped decisively by the history, politics, economics, and wider religious movements of a particular place and time.

At its founding, a congregation may relate faith to context in a variety of ways. In Puritan New England, for example, a minister would travel to an area previously unsettled by Europeans, build a church, and establish a town around it. One might say that faith created context in those places, though we must remember that the Puritan movement had itself emerged from the turbulent English context, and that this "new" land was already an inhabited landscape when those English settlers arrived. In 18th-century Philadelphia, faith opposed context when freed blacks—refusing to be segregated from the rest of the faithful—walked out of their home congregation and founded a church that would mother the whole new African Methodist Episcopal denomination. In the years after World War II, with the rise of the "automobile suburb," a brand new context engendered a new kind of congregation. Physically separated from the urban worlds of work and politics, the suburban church focused intensively on family and personal concerns. In each of these three examples, a spark of energy ignited the life of the new congregation—a spark struck from the encounter between faith and context.

If faith and context interact to release energy and create something new at the beginning of a congregation's life, the corollary proposition is not so comforting. As the community changes, congregations may simply keep doing what they did at the energized founding moment. In that case, the lively dance between congregation and context gets steadily slower, more distant, and more awkward until the church abandons the dance altogether. The building may still stand on the corner as a dusty relic, a club for the few who remember the good old days, or a fortress with barbed wire to keep the energy of the context from breaking in. But the central dynamic that gives a congregation its vitality has ceased.

Size transitions are critical because they present the congregation with an opportunity to adjust the connection between faith and context, to realign the inner life of the congregation with external realities brimming with potential for ministry. Numbers are secondary, but important; used well, statistics alert us to changes in the real lives and real relationships that make up congregations and communities. The primary issue in a time of size transition is suppleness—the congregation's ability to keep dancing with its context, to learn the new steps and rhythms that will carry it from one era of vitality to the next. Like learning a whole new style of dance, this process is often hard work and it is certainly not always pretty.

ANXIETY AND ENERGY

Often, congregations begin to explore the issues of size transition when leaders notice that the topic of numerical growth is generating a great deal of apprehension. Whether the congregation is small (up to about 150 in attendance), medium-sized (up to about 400) or large (over 400)[1]—and whether it is growing or declining—anxiety seems to peak when the church is crossing the boundary from one size category to another.

One of these size transitions poses special difficulties. In congregations where the average weekend attendance has leveled off somewhere between 150 and 250 (all sabbath services, all ages) while the surrounding community continues to gain population, size-related anxieties run especially high. Congregations that remain stuck for years (even decades) at this particular transition point—which I will call the pastoral-to-program size plateau—seem to experience the most intense discomfort of all.

A certain amount of anxiety can energize a congregation to identify a challenge and mobilize for new learning. But when the anxiety level gets too high, we humans engage in what psychiatrist Ronald Heifetz calls "work avoidance."[2] In the face of distress, we deny the facts, we hide, we fight about peripheral matters, we throw our energy into manic activity that doesn't really address the situation. Most of all, we demand that leaders "fix it" for us.

Wise congregational leaders resist this mandate. Instead, they build a "holding environment" to help members to manage anxiety about size change; then they give the hard work—connecting faith with context in a new way— back to the congregation "at a pace they can stand."[3] This book is intended to help you and others to fulfill both of these leadership tasks: to create a secure enough environment for learning, and to involve members with challenging choices about bringing faith to bear in a changing world.

How to Use This Book

For an individual reader, chapters 1 through 3 of this volume will provide concepts, research, strategies, and practical tools related to the pastoral-to-program size transition. But I hope you won't stop there. Chapter 4 provides a process designed to engage the congregation's whole leadership circle (defined broadly) in a shared learning experience and to produce a plan for further learning and action. Of course, that's an ambitious goal— even assuming that this is the right project for your congregation to undertake at this time. Let's think together about whether this is an appropriate resource for your church's situation.

The resources in this book were designed for congregations where:

- Average year-round attendance (all Sunday* services, all ages) has hit a plateau somewhere between 150 and 250 (i.e., between pastoral and program size).

---

*Congregations with Saturday evening or Sunday evening alternatives to Sunday morning worship should include unduplicated attendance at these services in their count. Children in education or nursery programs who do not participate in the main worship service should still be counted.

- The congregation is located in a context favorable to numerical growth. Likely indicators might be continuing population growth in the surrounding community and/or steady increases in total church membership while attendance remains stuck at a constant level.
- The congregation regularly attracts first-time visitors to Sunday worship.
- Both the pastor and lay opinion leaders believe that the congregation may be called to "step up" to the next size, and wish to engage in discernment and planning.
- Basic trust exists among pastor, lay leadership, and congregation.
- A small team of leaders can be found with the skills and motivation to guide others through a learning experience.

Other congregations will undoubtedly make use of the concepts and processes presented in this book. Simply bear in mind that I have organized this material for a particular audience—a set of congregations I have gotten to know through my consulting, training, and research.

THE LEARNING EXPERIENCE

The approach laid out in this book includes elements of education, discernment, and planning designed to occur over a period of about eight months. Though segments can be adapted for shorter time periods, I recommend that you sketch out in advance the entire process you will undertake and set firm dates for the key meetings. A definite plan of learning helps create a sturdy "holding environment"—framing a space in which people have agreed to stick with the subject and to avoid premature decisions.

The content in chapter 2 and the process described in chapter 4 are based on a pilot Alban course called "Raising the Roof," conducted online in the spring of 2001. I am profoundly grateful to the 12 congregations that participated in this cutting-edge work, and to the Massachusetts Conference of the United Church of Christ for underwriting a substantial portion of the cost.

The findings in chapter 3 resulted from my study of transition issues with seven UCC congregations in southeastern Massachusetts in the spring of 2000. I extend my thanks to them, and to the Massachusetts Conference, for their faithfulness and openness in this work of learning and growth.

CHAPTER 1

Changing Size

O ver the past two decades, the Alban Institute has based a good deal of its work with congregations on several observations about size:[1]

- Congregations fall into distinctive size categories, and congregations of different sizes organize in different ways. Each has its own recognizable way of "being church."
- Average sabbath attendance—all ages, all Saturday evening or Sunday worship services combined, over the whole year—is the best single indicator of size for Christian congregations.
- Congregations do not grow or decline smoothly, but tend to "plateau" at certain predictable levels of attendance.
- In order to break through an attendance plateau, a congregation must deliberately relinquish familiar patterns of behavior and begin to act as larger congregations act.

These descriptions of congregational dynamics relate to a growing body of theory about the way human beings organize themselves.[2] Humans tend to form primary groups of 12 or so, and clans of about 50. At about 150, a qualitative shift (the "tipping point") occurs and a true organization comes into being with official roles and structures, formal communication, and explicit procedures. Larger organizations seem to work best when built of combinations of these natural-sized groups.

In the literature of congregation development, any of these three natural-sized groups might be referred to as a "cell," though authors apply that term in different ways. When church growth specialist Gary McIntosh speaks of a "single cell" church, he means a congregation that has not yet passed the tipping point and become a true organization; for him, the term "cell" corresponds roughly to the natural social unit of 150 of fewer.[3] When church sociologist Arlin Rothauge talks about cells, he means extended networks of family and friendship no bigger than about 50 people.[4] When consultant Carl George recommends that a church organize itself into cell groups, he means units no bigger than 12 meeting for "fellowship, accountability, instruction and identity."[5]

SIZE CATEGORIES

The numerical thresholds of 50 and 150 underlie the particular size theory most often used by Alban in its work with churches—a framework originally developed by Arlin Rothauge. Rothauge uses four names for church sizes, described below (see figure 1).

Figure 1
Size Categories

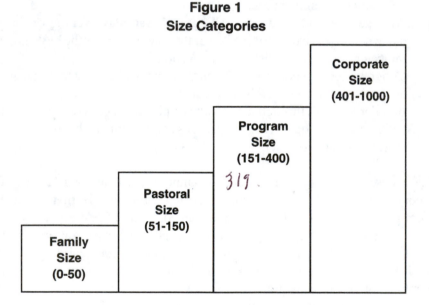

Family-size church (up to 50 adults and children at worship): A small congregation that operates like an extended family (and may in fact *be* a biological family network). Just as in the famous tavern from the television series *Cheers*, "everybody knows your name." This church is organized around one or two anchoring figures called matriarchs and patriarchs by Rothauge to indicate their tacit authority in the system. Such congregations often have part-time pastors, and their clergy tend to adopt a chaplain role— leading worship and giving pastoral care. A pastor who challenges the authority of a patriarch or matriarch, or who presumes to be the primary leader of the congregation, generally will not stay long.

Pastoral-size church (51 to 150): A coalition of two or three family and friendship networks unified around the person and role of the pastor. Clergy time is largely taken up maintaining a direct pastoral relationship with each member, coordinating the work of a small leadership circle, personally conducting worship, and leading small-group programs such as Bible study. The governing board usually operates like a committee, arranging much of the day-to-day life of the congregation. Members recognize each other's faces, know most people's names, and will notice if someone new is present at worship.

Program-size church (151 to 400): Known for the quality and variety of its programs. Separate programs for children, youth, couples, seniors, and other age and interest groups provide entry points for a wide range of people. The pastor's crucial role is to recruit, equip, and inspire a small circle of key program leaders—lay and ordained, paid and unpaid. This ring of leadership might include, for example, the choir director, the church school superintendent, the youth group leader, the coordinator of lay visitors, and the head of a committee that tracks new member incorporation. Working as a team with the pastor, they reach out to involve others as program participants and as leaders. Decision making is broadly distributed within the wider leadership circle (perhaps 50 people) and pastoral care is shared by laity. While Rothauge originally identified the maximum attendance for program size as 350, I will be using a higher figure of 400.[6]

Corporate-size church (401 to 1000): Known for excellence in worship and music, and for the range and diversity of its programs. Specialized ministries are provided for narrowly identified groups of people; several of these programs may be known beyond the congregation for their excellence. Often, distinct subcongregations form around multiple worship services. The senior pastor spends more time preparing to preach and lead worship than most clergy and must be skilled at working with a diverse staff of full-time professional leaders. Decision making is carried out by a multi-layered structure of staff, boards, and committees. While clergy continue to provide pastoral care, especially in crisis moments, most members find their spiritual support in small groups or from lay visitors. About a third of the corporate-size churches in the National Congregations Study[7] have at least 10 ongoing groups in addition to their classes, committees, and choirs. (Though the NCS did not collect actual attendance numbers, I believe that the 250 to 499 range of "regular attendees including children"—a size estimate provided by each congregation's respondent—roughly corresponds to "program size,"[8] and that the 500 to 999 range roughly corresponds to "corporate size.")

The first three of these size categories—family, pastoral, and program—include the vast majority (perhaps 90 percent[9]) of American congregations, but not the majority of church attenders. According to the National Congregations Study, half of those who participate regularly in the life of a congregation are found in congregations with 400 or more regular participants.[10] Some practitioners are calling these largest congregations "resource churches." Not all congregations over 400 are the same "size"; Carl George offers further categories labeled super-church (attendances of 1,000 to 3,000), mega-church (3,000 to 10,000) and meta-church (10,000 and beyond).

Let's look a little more closely at the character of the program-size church, using a few findings gleaned from the data set of National Congregations Study.

*   *The impression of intense activity in the program church is verified.* Most program-size churches (about 60 percent) have at least 10 ongoing classes for children or adults; a similar proportion of program-size churches report at least four other ongoing groups—besides committees and musical ensembles. About 70 percent of program-size churches have at least two choirs or musical groups.
*   *Remarkably, program-size churches have about the same number of committees as corporate-size churches.*[11] In each category, about half the churches have 4 to 10 functioning committees. Another third

of the churches in each group have an even more extensive organizational structure with 11 or more committees.

- *The program-size church, however, draws from a noticeably smaller pool of leaders to support a similar number of committees*, not to mention all the other activities that require leadership. About two-thirds of corporate-size churches have 50 or more attendees serving in some sort of leadership role—a fairly good talent pool in relation to the typical number of committees. On the other hand, almost half the program-size churches report fewer than 50 attendees serving in leadership roles of any sort.
- *Two-thirds of program-size churches operate with no more than three full-time paid staff of any kind.* This figure highlights another aspect of the size dilemma—lots of people and activities to manage but few full-time staff to handle the load. About 40 percent of all churches of this size make extensive use of part-time workers to fill out the staff roster (funding four to 24 part-time positions).

Gary McIntosh's term "stretched cell"[12] captures the feeling of this bind experienced by many midsized congregations—with activity and structure expanding faster than the resources required to support them.

GLASS CEILING

Between sizes, churches that have been growing steadily tend to hit an attendance plateau. Often they notice a mismatch between their flat year-to-year attendance chart and their other measures of growth—the number of visitors, members, or dollars contributed may keep increasing while attendance remains stuck.

Sometimes an attendance plateau is determined primarily by community demographics. In an isolated rural community with a fixed population, virtually every resident may have a well-established pattern of religious participation (or nonparticipation); life passages such as birth, marriage, childbearing, illness, and bereavement provide the primary openings for new or deeper relationship with God. Here a faithful, lively, and inviting congregation might take in or reactivate just enough members each year to replace those who die or move away.

Sometimes a flat attendance line is caused primarily by physical factors. For example, a worship service will tend to stop growing when 80 percent of the desirable seats are occupied on a regular basis. Because cultural norms about acceptable interpersonal distance are being violated, newcomers won't come back, or current members will attend less frequently. (When you calculate capacity, exclude inferior seating areas where regular members would never want to sit, and remember that these norms change from time to time; today's worshipers will probably feel cramped if they have less than 30 to 36 inches of space.) Some churches can break through an attendance plateau simply by adding more seating capacity, more parking spaces, or an additional service.

In contrast to plateaus created solely by community demographics or physical space limitations, the glass-ceiling effect of a size transition will occur even when there are lots of unchurched people around and plenty of seats left. Growth in attendance levels off because of a shortage in "sociological space"—the way the congregation arranges its life will simply not support the sustained involvement of more people than it already has. These size-related plateaus tend to be more mysterious to members and leaders because the causes are less visible and more cumulative in nature. At the boundary between sizes, many different hindrances converge to prevent the assimilation of new members and the full participation of those already on the rolls.

THE PASTORAL-TO-PROGRAM PLATEAU ZONE

The simplified diagram of size categories in figure 1 implies that the boundary between sizes is a sharp line—that, for example, the fifty-first person automatically pushes a congregation from family into pastoral size. This is hardly the case. In fact, we see a "plateau zone" between one size and the next—a band in which attendance tends to wobble up and down until there is a definite move to the next size. The church whose attendance data is charted below saw an initial spurt of growth that matched the growth in its surrounding community in the late sixties. Attendance then dropped back into a plateau zone and stayed there for about 20 years, in spite of continued population growth in the town (see figure 2).

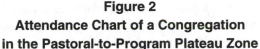

Figure 2
Attendance Chart of a Congregation
in the Pastoral-to-Program Plateau Zone

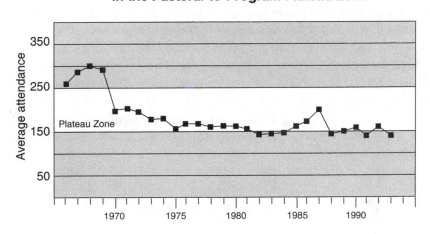

My recent research (reported in chapter 3) suggests that the pastoral-to-program plateau may occur anywhere between about 150 and 250. Churches with attendance in this zone often give an impression of being quite unsettled about which size they really want to be. Here are some typical expressions of that ambivalence:

- While the pastor and evangelism committee work hard on growth and welcome, members frequently say that it would be best to remain small so that we can all know each other.
- Growth plans are presented primarily as medicine to cure a budget squeeze; leaders hesitate to say that the congregation might have a vocation to reach more people.
- Though members describe the church as welcoming to newcomers, leaders hear many complaints about plans to add capacity; for example, by adding a worship service, expanding the staff, or buying land for parking.

Life in this zone is a lot like straddling the San Andreas Fault: you can make better decisions if you know not only where the rifts occur, but also what deeper movements of the earth are driving the surface eruption. It is true that congregations are changing and adjusting all the time; dozens of different factors are in play, moving in subtle gradations that make any size theory look oversimplified. Still, some of the forces at work are more powerful than others, more determinative of relationships and results. A two-dimensional model of size change helps to clarify the lines of demarcation.

One dimension of change, shown along the bottom of the chart, is described by the terms *organism* and *organization*. The vertical dimension is described by the terms *pastor-centered* and *group-centered*. As congregations move among Rothauge's four sizes (family, pastoral, program, and corporate) they follow an N-shaped path across the fault lines (see figure 3).

Figure 3
Size Transition "N-Curve"

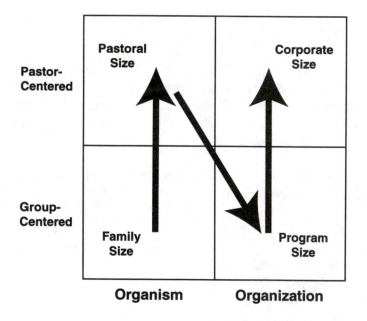

Organism versus Organization

Family- and pastoral-size churches resemble an organism more than an organization. Congregations of these two sizes tend to be relatively homogeneous in make-up. Each revolves around a central relationship that can be apprehended immediately and intuitively: the familial bond among the members (family-size church) or the dyadic relationship between the sole ordained leader and the congregation (pastoral-size church). The congregation's identity is largely inherent in these central relationships. Ask the question, "Who are you as a church?" in a family-size congregation, and someone will probably introduce you around the whole circle of members. Ask that question in a pastoral-size church, and someone will most likely tell you about the congregation's relationship with its pastor, often symbolized by the rapport (or lack thereof) between pastor and board. In these two smaller sizes, the notion that a congregation might choose or shape an identity intentionally would probably seem odd; its identity is more of a "given" to be preserved and defended.

In program- and corporate-size churches, on the other hand, the variety and complexity of relationships require conscious attention to matters of identity, purpose, structure, role of leaders, and so on. Neither the members nor the pastor can intuitively grasp the wholeness of the system. The larger membership and the rich variety of programming will only cohere well if leaders "construct" a clear identity for the church and express it consciously in a mission statement, a vision, or a strategic plan. For newcomers raised in a smaller church, this work of construction may seem taxing and bureaucratic. On the other hand, the intentionality of the larger congregation in discerning God's purpose might stimulate their imagination about church life, clarify their reasons for participating, and provide rich networks of friendship, growth, and ministry.

The distinction between organism and organization is not absolute. Small congregations are still subject to the laws that govern not-for-profit corporations in the United States, and may be subject to lawsuits if they do not attend well to organizational matters like employment agreements, financial accountability, and policies for child protection. Larger congregations are still living systems held together by subtly balanced forces that we may only dimly perceive. Nevertheless, the difference between the two emphases is usually palpable.

GROUP-CENTERED VERSUS PASTOR-CENTERED

The movement from family to pastoral size (the upward arrow on the left-hand side of the chart) involves a change in the way the system centers its life. The family-size church feels like a tribe or a "committee of the whole." Not everyone on the committee has equal influence, to be sure, but the single circle of members works things through in its own characteristic way. A student minister or short-term pastor who tries to take charge of that tribe is in for a rude awakening because a family-size church does not usually revolve around the clergy.

When attendance exceeds 50, the congregation encounters a crisis—the unbroken circle of members no longer works well as the defining constellation of the congregation's life. Members experience distress because they can no longer keep track of all the relationships. According to anthropologist Robin Dunbar, this discomfort has a biological basis in the limited capacity of primate neural networks;[13] we humans can only keep track of a certain number of face-to-face relationships in a given social system. In order to grow further, the system must allow the development of two or three different networks of family and fellowship—each of a mentally manageable size—and it must establish a symbolic center around which those networks can orient themselves. Typically, it becomes "pastor-centered."

A great deal has been written about the dangers of clerical domination in churches, and many have questioned whether this shift to a pastor-centered system is desirable at all. I would not equate "pastor-centered" with "pastor-dominated." The research of Speed Leas and George Parsons suggests that a greater proportion of members may actually participate in decisions at pastoral size than at family size. It may be that the heightened role of the pastor in relation to the board moves the congregation's political center from the kitchen table to a more accessible public setting and requires that the ordained and elected leaders work as a team to move projects forward. The pastor's central position as communication switchboard also allows for a great deal of informal consultation and problem solving. He or she can monitor key relationships (noticing when people are tense with each other, for example), initiate needed conversations, and anticipate likely clashes.

As attendance approaches 150, however, the congregation must become more group-centered once again because the pastor can no longer carry around the whole system in his or her head. There are too many individual pastoral needs to track. The relationships among projects and leaders are becoming too complex to be coordinated solely through board discussion and pastoral diplomacy. A new kind of teamwork becomes necessary in an uneven matrix of leadership where some programs have paid staff, some have volunteer leaders so dedicated that they function like staff, and some have committees at the helm. Board and pastor must find ways to keep the parts connected with each other *directly* (in horizontal networks of collaboration) not just *indirectly* through board reports and liaisons. As in a spider web, the center of this leadership network does not consist of a single point (the pastor) but a small circle (half a dozen key program leaders—paid and unpaid, clergy and lay) led by the pastor.

In the move to program size, clergy must shift a good deal of their time and attention away from direct delivery of pastoral care toward assembling and guiding that team of program leaders. They must also find ways to offer spiritual enrichment to the board, whose job has become much more demanding. Skills for this kind of group-oriented ministerial leadership have not usually been emphasized in seminary or employed as primary selection criteria in the ordination process. Hence, many clergy find themselves poorly equipped for a pastoral-to-program transition.

To make things worse, this breakdown of the pastor-centered way of being church occurs at the same time as the shift from organism to organization. The congregation is now traversing the diagonal portion of the N-shaped path, crossing both the horizontal and vertical fault lines simultaneously. The pastoral-to-program change is doubly discontinuous.

In the corporate-size congregation, the need for more pastor-centered leadership emerges once again (note the vertical line on the right hand side of the chart). The program church's lively but lumpy network of staff, volunteer program heads, and committees can no longer provide the overview and strategic direction the system needs. At corporate size, complex networks of coordination are still required, but the central pastor must begin to project a large enough symbolic presence (through preaching, presiding, leading the board, and heading the expanded staff) to unify a diverse and energetic community. To be effective, this high-profile leader must find a reliable way to maintain spiritual perspective and must use the aura of headship to help the whole system grapple with its core identity and purpose.

ESCAPING THE PASTORAL-TO-PROGRAM PLATEAU ZONE

In the pastoral-to-program plateau zone, many different hindrances converge to prevent the assimilation of new members and the full participation
of those already on the rolls. In the next chapter, we will examine in more
detail the passive barriers that keep congregations stuck at this particular
level.

CHAPTER 2

Barriers to Growth

Numerically static congregations in growing communities usually see themselves as open and welcoming. They feel successful if they quickly "replace" the members they lose to death, relocation, or discontent. But they are typically reluctant—or at best ambivalent—about expanding capacity in ways that would permit net growth. To refrain from creating needed capacity is to post an effective "no vacancy" sign. Many newcomers will get the message and go away. A few who are more determined will find their way into the system, but an addition will always be balanced by the departure (or less frequent attendance) of someone else.

PASSIVE BARRIERS

I would define a passive barrier as an unacknowledged hindrance to growth and welcome. Think for a moment about a physical analogy—handicap access. A congregation may be proud of the blue sign that reserves a parking space and the new ramp that leads to the front entrance, yet no one with a wheelchair or walker attends more than once, leading the congregation to conclude (with some disappointment) that people with disabilities just aren't interested. Looking closer, we might find that the bathrooms are located down a flight of steps in the fellowship hall. The explicit message (disabled people are welcome) is contradicted by the implicit message (we're not able or willing to provide everything a disabled person needs in order to attend). This same split between avowed intention and actual behavior may apply to many aspects of church life in a congregation that has hit a size plateau—especially if that congregation is located in a growing community. Let's examine six passive barriers to numerical growth that keep churches stuck in the pastoral-to-program plateau zone.

Barrier 1:
We are unclear whether we have a vocation to make room for more
of our neighbors in order to serve a growing community.

A major Lutheran-sponsored research study[1] placed congregations in three
broad groupings—classified according to the way pastors and lay opinion
leaders described the congregation's sense of purpose or calling.

In group A (perhaps 20 to 30 percent of U.S. churches), leaders had
an outward focus and viewed their congregation as a mission outpost. "While
meeting the needs of their current members, they also seek ways to communicate with people who are not currently active in their ministry," and to
share their historic faith in the midst of cultural change. While they are not
primarily focused on numbers, these churches do make the changes required to reach and serve the community around them—including, we may
infer, such expansion of physical and organizational capacity as might be
needed in a growing community.

In group B1 (perhaps 30 to 40 percent of U.S. churches) were congregations "interested" in ministering to those beyond their current membership but lacking a firm plan, appropriate methods, and the willingness to
change practices that might be hindering outreach. Churches in group B2
(perhaps 40 percent) were primarily committed to "strengthening their current members."

When these subgroups were compared, congregations in group A were,
on the whole, "experiencing increases in the variety and depth of their ministry, increased financial support, . . . increases in members who were previously unchurched, and increases in membership." In contrast, churches in
group B (both subsets) saw "stability or decreases in financial support, increases in financial problems, few or no members who were previously
unchurched, increases in the average age of members, and decreases in
membership." In short, the critical characteristic of vital congregations (taking
into account several different measures of health) was their strong sense of
vocation to reach and serve those outside the church.

If your congregation has a weak sense of calling to reach out beyond
its current circle of members, attention to the five more technical barriers
described below will probably not result in a breakthrough to the next size.
In chapter 3, we will consider why mainline churches sometimes have a
hard time generating passion for invitational outreach in particular.

Barrier 2:
We are unclear about size plateau concepts or realities.

A congregation that has seen steady, incremental growth in attendance is very likely to hit a mysterious barrier (a "glass ceiling") when it moves into the pastoral-to-program plateau zone. Many members will initially assume that new people can join if they really want to—after all, there are usually some new faces in church—and will be baffled by leaders who announce that major change is needed. Though some lay leaders may never embrace the "glass ceiling" concept, I have seen many light up with recognition and relief when they see why the church isn't growing and hear that other congregations are having the same experience.

Still, new concepts only constitute half of the equation. Even people who grasp the idea of a predictable size plateau may not have an accurate view of what is happening numerically in the congregation. Very few churches have at their fingertips a 30-year attendance chart that most lay leaders will accept as an accurate picture. When someone begins to gather information, there is almost invariably a lively debate about the accuracy and meaning of the numbers. This debate is a sign that the congregation is developing new learning about itself—clearing up vague or false impressions about its numerical track record.

Where reliable counts are missing, it is very freeing to call upon a group of leaders to develop their "best estimate" for each particular year (or era), and to identify the assumptions and impressions upon which that estimate is based. After each volley of debate about what might be true, leaders will need to press the group once more: "So what number should I write down as our best estimate for this particular period?" This work can feel like pulling teeth, but the result is powerful: a shared view of the congregation's past.

The gathering of attendance information usually sparks an even deeper debate about what is truly desired. "Do we want quantity or quality?" "We're not like those other churches that focus on growth for growth's sake." "We're not on an ego trip." Here again is the question of vocation. Is your congregation called to reach out (in *both* invitation and service) to its neighbors? Can you embrace average sabbath attendance as *one* (not the only) measure of how well you are responding to the needs of a growing community? As a leader poses these questions, it is important to encourage the exploration of different points of view and notice which statements tend to stop the conversation dead. By creating an environment that helps an avoided conversation to go forward, you may find that some previously blocked energy begins to flow. Respectful argument about important issues is a sign of congregational health.

Barrier 3:
Our space is effectively "filled up."

Although size plateaus will occur when there is still ample physical capacity (simply because the scale of the social system has changed), most congregations in a size transition can identify at least one aspect of physical capacity that is seriously overtaxed. Likely candidates include worship seating, parking, education space (children and adults), fellowship gathering places, and offices areas.

Worship space is effectively "filled up" when 80 percent of the desirable seats are full on any regular basis. Yes, an assertive person could walk up to the front pew or climb over several people to take that seat in the center of the row, but there are good reasons those seats remain empty when the rest of the church is full (just think about the way seats fill in a movie theater). Most of us would rather be near the end of a row and a little further back, even if we know our fellow congregants pretty well. So imagine how the newcomer feels if squeezing in or parading up to the front appear to be the only choices (seats that may not even be visible from the entrance). When your main worship service reaches 80 percent of comfortable capacity (measured at 30 to 36 inches per person), you may be pretty certain that you are discouraging frequent attendance by current members and presenting a "no vacancy" sign to newcomers.

Parking is "filled up" if there is no convenient space obvious to the newcomer who arrives five minutes before the service starts. Even on a good day, many long-established congregations present their new and existing members with a parking hassle. If the weather is bad, if the ground is soft underfoot, or if it's dark outside, much of their parking (on the street or in an unpaved lot, for example) becomes unacceptable to most visitors and to a good many members. I find that congregations are often well aware of the problem but have long since given up on finding any solution (perhaps they are wedged into a built-up area or are daunted by the price of an adjoining parcel). In fact, such a church does have options; for example, the addition of another major sabbath worship service. It may take considerable leadership skill to break through the congregation's sense of helplessness (and the denial that helplessness often generates) to mobilize a serious effort to remove the parking barrier.

A shortage of education, fellowship, or office space can also create a cramped, unwelcoming environment. Parents today have high standards for children's programming and form strong impressions about quality from the look of the facility. Social hour is difficult at best for many visitors and becomes totally unappealing if there isn't even a visible path to the coffee pot. Crowded and poorly designed office areas diminish staff productivity and professionalism, communicating a negative message about the congregation's capacity to serve its members and neighbors.

Barrier 4:
We are not staffed for growth.

In the middle of pastoral size (a total attendance of 100 to 120 people), congregations are often staffed by a full-time ordained minister, a half-time secretary, a part-time maintenance person or cleaning service, and a musician who is compensated for a day or two each week to prepare instrumental music and rehearse the choir for one main service. When attendance exceeds about 120, this staffing model starts straining a bit to accommodate new members and new ministries. (The percentage of congregational resources required to maintain this pattern has risen dramatically during the 30 years since I started seminary, because of improvements in clergy compensation and sharp rises in insurance costs.)

At an average attendance of 150, a congregation that wants to support continued growth may add a half-time position on the program side (assisting pastor or lay professional), increase the level of office support, and extend a custodian's hours for building maintenance and room setup. Having launched a children's choir or a new adult ensemble, the church may budget for an additional day of its musician's time. As attendance approaches 200, growth often cannot be sustained without (the equivalent of) at least two full-time program staff (clergy or lay), full-time office support, and a half- to full-time custodian.

Many congregations carry a single mental model for adding staff: calling a young minister, right out of seminary, to handle church school and

youth group, along with some liturgical and pastoral duties. I wonder if this
has ever worked very well. Relatively few new clergy feel a strong call to
minister primarily with children and youth, and even these two related are-
nas require different talents. Women clergy may be sensitive about repli-
cating old stereotypes (women work with children), and ordination in midlife
is now the norm rather than the exception. Many midsized congregations
have tried this "young minister for young members" model, experienced a
breakdown, and then moved toward more creative staffing concepts. In
several cases I have studied recently, the lay leader (often a female) who
headed the education committee during the search for an assisting minister,
was eventually brought onto the paid staff as the part-time director of
children's education after the recently added clergy position did not fulfill
expectations.

In general, staffing through the pastoral-to-program transition requires
a great deal of flexibility and "outside the box" thinking. Instead of a single
professional with disparate responsibilities, transitional churches often multiply part-time positions that are filled by locally available laity and clergy
with a special talent for a single task. When retired or bivocational clergy
reside in the vicinity, growing churches may contract with them for limited
pieces of pastoral or programmatic work, instead of creating a more conventional ministerial position. Often, at least one paid educational or administrative position is filled by a member of the congregation.

Hiring members is a tricky venture. It is harder to maintain clear lines
of accountability when a staff member occupies other social roles in the
system such as church member, long-time friend, or relative. Boundaries
get fuzzy; for example, with whom should I discuss the ups and downs of
the last staff meeting, or where am I free to complain if I hated that new
hymn? Hiring of members only works in a healthy way when the employed
person willingly relinquishes most of the prerogatives of "member" (e.g., "I
may express an opinion on any issue") in favor of behaviors appropriate to
the "staff member" role ("I voice concerns in staff meetings, then support
the staff decision").

Just as important as the right *amount* of paid staff is the *role* a church
staff member is expected to play. Unless a church has a huge endowment
to call upon, employing someone to "do" each ministry is not a feasible
approach—and isn't the wisest strategy even if the church can afford it.
To open up the potential for continued growth, a congregation on the pastoral-to-program size plateau needs staff whose priority (and talent) is releasing gift-based member ministry rather than "delivering" all the ministry as

solo performers. This can be a difficult shift, not only for clergy (who have generally been selected and trained for solo performance as preacher, teacher, counselor) but also for many church musicians and youth leaders (who may derive their deepest satisfaction from doing rather than equipping).

Such a role shift is usually difficult for the congregation as well. It may seem self-evident to parents that the church needs a talented youth minister to inspire and involve their teenagers. The board of deacons, observing that the senior pastor doesn't have much time to call on shut-ins, may recommend a part-time "minister of visitation" position. A third group of members, seeking more adult education and spiritual enrichment, may press for the call of a full-time associate minister. While the congregation could seek a person with the right talents to address one or more of these needs personally, it might more profitably examine the strategies employed by growing congregations to activate and support creative member ministry in each of these areas. Increased staffing is still needed, but the congregation with an emphasis on member ministry will look for the candidate who knows how to build an energized team of adult youth mentors, train and supervise lay pastoral visitors, or build an extensive network of small groups for spiritual growth. A new staff position aimed at strengthening member ministry might not, in fact, be program specific at all; instead, the congregation could add a talented person to work across the board with volunteer development, including year-round work with members on discovering and activating their spiritual gifts.

Many congregations struggle with the question of *when* to add staff. Usually, the answer lies somewhere between "build staff and growth will come" and "not until we have every cent in hand." If a new staff position is strategically focused to reach unchurched neighbors and activate peripheral members, it may be reasonable to launch the position when you have raised 50 percent of its funding for the first year to 18 months.[2] While it is certainly possible to expand staff too fast, most transitional churches either wait too long or lack a clear strategy showing how this position will help the congregation to reach out beyond the circle of people who currently participate.

As a congregation reassesses the size and role of its paid staff, office equipment should also be reviewed, including computer hardware and software, telephones, and message systems. Training may be needed if staff members are to make full use of these ministry resources.

Barrier 5:
Our concept of an "adequate" budget does not permit growth.

As attendance passes the 150 mark, a church budget that previously grew in modest increments may now step up rather sharply because of the change in scale. Lay leaders responsible for the budgeting process may experience tremendous anxiety as they hear fellow members express hesitation, or even predict catastrophe, with regard to church finances. A pastor frustrated with a nervous board may be tempted to charge slow moving leaders with lack of faith.

Instead of stretching old financial assumptions a little farther each year (until they snap!), it may be helpful to form a special study committee to look at the whole budget picture in relation to size. Just as an assessor might identify "comparables" (similar properties) when determining the market value of a home, church leaders can develop a list of congregations that seem like peers in terms of size and community setting. Several of the congregations should be churches of your own denomination, but it can also be helpful to step outside the frame of your own particular tradition. Find out about each congregation's total operating budget, the percentages allocated to various purposes, and its approach to staffing, stewardship, and capital improvements. The purpose of such a study is not to find one right model, but rather, to define a budget range and a set of practices for thoughtful comparison.

Once this assessment has occurred, an overall financial strategy can be developed that includes a variety of elements (some not strictly "financial" but powerfully related):

- Communicating a clear vision about where the congregation is headed
- Clarifying the key steps needed in order to realize that vision
- Building spiritual commitment to proportional giving (a percentage of one's total income) as the basis of the annual pledge
- Incorporating new members effectively (including orientation about giving)
- Connecting members to hands-on ministries related to their spiritual gifts
- Sending trained visitors to reach out in caring ministry to lapsed members within three months of the time they stop attending or sharply reduce their participation

- Raising funds to increase the capacity and quality of the physical plant (including worship seating, nursery and education space, parking, signage, and hospitality areas) through well-conceived capital campaigns
- Teaching planned giving (naming the church in one's will) as a spiritual practice

Barrier 6:
Our ministry infrastructure is inadequate for movement to the next size.

In the transition to program size, a paradox arises. Everyone wants to retain the congregation's personal touch, but without excellent organizational machinery, that personal touch will be impossible to achieve. Developing infrastructure in the following areas enables the congregation to provide reliable (and personal) ministry to new and existing members.

New Member Incorporation. In the transition to program size, the congregation can no longer expect the pastor to ensure that each new person or household finds a suitable place within the life of the church. It now takes a team of three or four people with diverse talents to design and manage a coherent process of new member incorporation. (Many more will be involved in the face-to-face ministries of incorporation, such as greeting, visiting, teaching newcomer's classes, but all of those people need coordination, role clarity, and emotional support to sustain their welcoming work.) Ideally, this team is headed by a motivated lay person who has attended a training workshop and done some reading on the subject. Instead of allowing this leadership position to change as committees rotate, consider making this an appointed position; in effect, an unpaid staff position with a position description and a voice, at least periodically, in staff meetings. (Unpaid staff positions may also be needed to develop the other kinds of infrastructure described below.)

Member Ministry Development. Sometimes this function has been called volunteer management, but innovative congregations object to the shotgun approach to recruitment usually implied by the word *volunteer*. Rather, they identify the gifts required for a ministry and reach out to specific people whose passions and talents match the need. And they work the other way as well: they look at the giftedness of their members in order to determine what ministries the congregation might fruitfully undertake. Many congregations have experimented over the years with some form of "time and talent survey," but I rarely meet a leader who tells me that this method produced the desired results (at least by itself). In order to make a serious connection between member gifts and member ministries, the congregation must commit itself to a year-round strategy of interactive gift exploration aimed at spiritual growth and joyful service, rather than simply filling slots. Interactive methods include one-to-one interviewing, one-day workshops, or short courses.

Gift identification strategies often fail because they try to involve the whole congregation at once. It is wiser to begin by finding a few members with two special gifts: interviewing skills and passion for releasing the gifts of others. Ask them to start conducting one-to-one interviews with newcomers. As this team develops appropriate methods, expand the program by inviting some current members to be interviewed about their gifts. (Include people who might be good candidates to serve on a gift identification team later on—as interviewers or workshop leaders). Include an evening or two of gift identification activities in your adult "foundations" course (see below), so that this work is seen as a natural element of adult education. As you go along, make sure that each person receives a follow-up interaction, linking gifts with specific ministries. People might be invited personally to participate in a specific ministry within the church; encouraged to join an appropriate community service group; or recognized for the ministry through which their gift is already joyfully exercised in their family, in civic participation, or at work. (On a particular Sunday, for example, prayers of the people might include thanksgiving for particular members who exercise healing gifts in medicine, nursing, volunteering with a rape crisis center, or caring for an elderly parent.) As you can see, this year-round strategy will need to be headed by a gifted lay leader or part-time staff person whose passion and talent is for releasing the ministries of all the members.

Adult Faith Formation. Many pastoral-size churches deepen the faith of adults mainly through a program of Sunday forums and perhaps an adult Bible study group. This probably didn't work too badly in days past, when people usually stayed within their childhood faith tradition and when public schools exposed students to Christian scriptures and holy days. Today, this approach produces congregations of people who are uncertain and inarticulate about their faith. A cornerstone of an adult formation strategy is a "foundations course": a reintroduction to Christian faith and practice for all adults in the congregation (not just converts or newcomers). There are many curricula from which a congregation may choose; the particular material is not nearly as important as the strategy of which it is a part. Appendix A in this book provides some suggestions about elements of an adult formation strategy (which might also include small groups and member ministry development).

Pastoral Care. A full transition from pastoral to program size requires that clergy, lay leaders, and congregation renegotiate expectations about pastoral care. In the middle of pastoral size, members usually expect that their minister will become personally involved with their moments of joy, crisis, and transition. At a subconscious level, the presence of their clergy may symbolize divine love and fidelity. So, when the sole pastor becomes less available to accompany each member personally through crucial passages, anxiety tends to rise and harsh judgments may be made about pastoral performance. Clergy themselves often feel they are failing their people, even when they understand intellectually that they must recognize their own limits.

Within this crisis of expectations lies an opportunity to reclaim "pastoral caring" as a task of the faith community, which delegates aspects of this ministry to its clergy and other staff. Many resources are available for training and guiding member teams to undertake various kinds of visitation (shut-ins, newcomers, lapsed members). Where the congregation has a well-developed pattern of small groups, much "pastoral caring" will occur naturally between members who know each other's stories because they gather regularly for prayer, study, and support.

Small-Group Ministries. The informal circle of fellowship at the center of a pastoral-size church can be the "blest . . . tie that binds" a limited number of people into strong relationship with the congregation. Once the slots in that network are filled up, newcomers entering the system (or inactive members looking for a closer connection) may experience a general friendliness, but are unlikely to make real friends—spiritual or social—until the congregation finds a way to multiply the circles of personal connection. Some newly formed congregations organize into "cells" right from the beginning; joining the congregation means joining a cell-group just as much as it means attending sabbath worship. Long-established congregations do not usually succeed in attempts to organize the whole membership into groupings of some uniform sort. But they can give conscious attention to the quality of group life by:

- Fostering a variety of small group opportunities for prayer, study, service and decision making
- Insuring that a new group is formed every year to 18 months (since new groups are the easiest for new people to join)
- Helping existing groups to become more permeable to new members
- Training and supporting group leaders
- Monitoring the climate of group life, and coaching leaders when problems arise
- Sponsoring some short-term small group experiences each year in which members may experiment with spiritual growth and the congregation may "try out" ideas for longer-term groups
- Helping groups close in a positive way when they have completed their arc of energy
- Enriching the life of committees with simple spiritual practices: storytelling, sharing of joys and concerns, asking group members to identify Bible passages or hymns that relate to work of the group

Board Development and Staff Team Development. In the transition to program size, the role of the governing board shifts away from hands-on management toward concern with overarching goals, policy, and oversight. Board orientation and training, periodic retreats to clarify the big picture, and use of consultants with appropriate expertise will help strengthen the board's capacity to guide the congregation's life. Similar resources are needed by a growing staff as it develops new teamwork patterns and learns to manage the growing complexity of ministry. Often, a senior pastor is now formally designated as "head of staff" to signal his or her responsibility to form the group into an effective team.

INFRASTRUCTURE AND OVERLOAD

In chapter 1, I noted the "stretched cell" phenomenon: the tendency of many midsized congregations to add activities and structures more quickly than they add new leaders. How do congregations break free from this bind?

First, don't equate involvement with church governance. A good many congregations see an extensive committee structure as the best way to release member gifts for ministry. For the GI generation, this wasn't such a bad strategy. These adults came out of World War II with high confidence in institutions and leaders. They knew how to join, participate in, and influence church organizations. Subsequent generations of adults (and even the GIs as they absorb attitudes of the wider culture) are less patient with institutional life. The "baby boom" generation tends to ask how church involvement will meet their personal needs. Though adults of the "baby bust" generation are more interested in family ties and community service, they don't enjoy endless committee conversation about these topics—they want to participate in meaningful action. Today's program-size churches do better when they have fewer, smaller standing committees but many more small teams, each passionate about a very particular ministry within the congregation or to the wider community. Both staff and standing committee members need skills for oversight and planning, and a passion for member ministry development, in order to open up opportunities for many different kinds of participation.

Second, identify the core of your member involvement strategy and build around that center. A church in the pastoral-to-program transition will become overwhelmed if it tries to build—all at once—all the kinds of infrastructure I have described. Here is an example of what I mean by "identifying the core" of your strategy.

Suppose a congregation decides that its member involvement strategy will be centered on *adult faith formation*. It expresses its passion for engaging adults in a shared exploration of faith by offering regularly a home-grown "foundations" course (see appendix A), the Alpha course, *Disciple* Bible study, Disciples of Christ in Community (DOCC), or some other comparable program.[3] Since this is a long-term strategy, leaders persistently build commitment and structure (such as a team of trained leaders for the course) to keep adult spiritual growth on the front burner. Over time, as a result of personal invitations and positive buzz, more and more adults in the congregation take part in the core faith development experience. When this number reaches about one-third of the active adult members, the congregation's culture "tips." Board meetings turn more regularly to questions of mission and include times of explicit spiritual discernment. Newcomers perceive the congregation's clear and positive faith identity, and they know how to "get in." Members become more confident about telling their own faith story as well as the congregation's. With adult faith development at the center of the infrastructure for member involvement, recruitment into the core course would be a key goal of new member ministry. Gift identification would begin during the course. And new ministry teams or sharing groups would be generated as each group "graduates" from the course, building on the relationships that have been generated.

Are you getting the idea? Instead of viewing your congregation's infrastructure as a collection of separate silos (or a set of plates you have to keep spinning!), you might see it as a wedge: an integrated effort with a leading edge that gives the strategy "bite" and leverage. In Southern Baptist congregations, large year-round adult Sunday school classes are often the leading edge of member involvement; these churches keep very close track of adult Sunday school attendance while only estimating the number at worship—the exact opposite of most mainline Protestant churches. Another candidate for the "leading edge" of a member involvement strategy might be small groups. For long-established mainline churches, small groups tend to be an enrichment option for "people who like that sort of thing," but some congregations decide that small groups will be the major vehicle by which key goals (spiritual growth, mutual care among members, gift identification, incorporating newcomers) will be accomplished. They employ staff with special talents for organizing small group ministry; they recruit their very best lay leaders to become small group facilitators; they study models from other churches and persist in learning from failures.

Third, take people's gifts more seriously. As congregations move into program size, activities and structures tend to expand faster than the pool of leaders. So one strategic move for a congregation in the plateau zone would be to make member ministry development (especially work on identifying and releasing gifts) a top priority. I have encountered few mainline congregations that have done much more than scratch the surface in the area of gifts. A time-and-talent survey at pledge time (rarely followed up with any care), and perhaps an occasional sermon or class, is the most one is likely to encounter. A leading writer on releasing gifts for ministry, Jean Morris Trumbauer, provides this diagnosis:

> Members of the Church of the Usual Ways attend church on Sundays, but their lives during the week often seem disconnected from what happens there. They find little at church that addresses their personal life struggles. It hasn't even occurred to most of them that their congregation could have a role to play in helping them sort out their purposes and direction in life; wrestle with issues of self-confidence, meaning, and change; or make choices about work, school, and volunteer service.
>
> The Church of the Usual Ways regularly asks for volunteers to support the church's programs. . . . The "Faithful Few" implement most of the programs of the congregation, and they are getting tired. But the congregation has no programs or processes to assist members to discover and develop their gifts, to discern their purpose and mission in life, or to learn how to apply their faith to their daily lives from Monday through Sunday.[4]

In spite of a stream of new literature in this field from the 1970s onward, Trumbauer concludes that mainline churches have not established "sustained approaches to assist members in discovering their gifts and calls to ministry in the world."

For churches that make small group ministry the center of member involvement, I would hope that serious work on gift identification—focused primarily on ministry in daily life and secondarily on ministry within the congregation—would be an ongoing part of group life. For the more typical mainline church where small groups are not the central strategy, I would like to share a dream.

When I arrive in your church as a newcomer, I am welcomed with information about the ways in which this congregation can help me to grow spiritually. Figure 4 below shows the flow chart in the orientation brochure.

Figure 4
A Faith Formation Framework

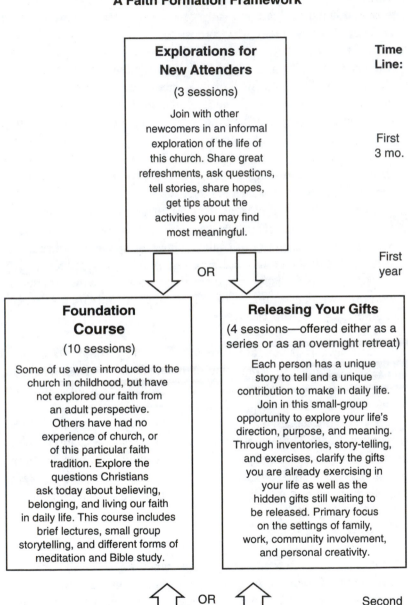

Explorations for New Attenders

(3 sessions)

Join with other newcomers in an informal exploration of the life of this church. Share great refreshments, ask questions, tell stories, share hopes, get tips about the activities you may find most meaningful.

OR

Foundation Course

(10 sessions)

Some of us were introduced to the church in childhood, but have not explored our faith from an adult perspective. Others have had no experience of church, or of this particular faith tradition. Explore the questions Christians ask today about believing, belonging, and living our faith in daily life. This course includes brief lectures, small group storytelling, and different forms of meditation and Bible study.

OR

Releasing Your Gifts

(4 sessions—offered either as a series or as an overnight retreat)

Each person has a unique story to tell and a unique contribution to make in daily life. Join in this small-group opportunity to explore your life's direction, purpose, and meaning. Through inventories, story-telling, and exercises, clarify the gifts you are already exercising in your life as well as the hidden gifts still waiting to be released. Primary focus on the settings of family, work, community involvement, and personal creativity.

Time Line:

First 3 mo.

First year

Second year

I sign up for the Exploration for New Attenders, where the leader suggests that I sign up for one of the two main courses within the first year, then the other course in the second year. She provides some clues about how to decide which course would be better for me to start with, based on my experiences, questions, and hopes. She gives me a 2-year calendar of specific dates for each course and a sign-up form to use if I would like to reserve a place.

I am relieved to find that the courses are offered in very flexible ways. The Foundations Course is broken down into three units of three classes each, plus an introductory dinner and orientation for all the participants; if I can't take the whole course this year, at least I can begin with the dinner and one unit of learning. The day and time each course is offered changes from year to year to provide options for people with different sorts of schedules. I was worried that the course might be cancelled if only six or seven of us signed up, but I discovered that the courses proceed as long as there are enough people for enjoyable group interaction.

The leader explains that the Releasing Your Gifts course doesn't focus mainly on volunteering in the congregation (that's a surprise!), but she does suggest some good ways to get involved. We fill out an inventory called "Discovering the Gifts of the People,"[5] designed to clarify our hopes for involvement in the congregation's ministry. It includes some surprising questions. Do I prefer to work alone or in a group? Do I prefer to lead or participate? Would I like an ongoing involvement or a one-time experience? Our leader introduces us to the Member Ministry Coordinator—an unpaid staff member who follows up with each of us based on what we have put on our inventory. This same person follows up with everyone who takes the Gifts Course to see how things are going as they experiment with new ways for releasing their giftedness. The Member Ministry Coordinator reminds us to say no if we are invited to serve in a way that isn't quite right for us—another surprise.

That's my dream. I believe such an approach to lie within the capacity of many of the transitional congregations I work with. Consult appendix B for resources you might use to undertake gift identification and member ministry development in your own church.

CHAPTER 3

Foundations for the Breakthrough to Program Size

Five years ago, a prestigious Boston medical school started to "raise the roof"—to build a brand new seventh floor atop an older, six-story building. Construction was well under way before the architects discovered, to their horror, that the existing structure was not strong enough to carry the weight of the new addition. Project leaders had to make a costly and embarrassing trip back to the drawing board. In this chapter, I will discuss four preparatory tasks that might keep a church—especially a mainline Protestant congregation in a growing community—from suffering the same fate as our Boston architects.

"Raising the Roof" Research Project

In June and July of 2000, I studied the experience of seven congregations—all UCC churches in southeastern Massachusetts—moving through the transition zone between pastoral and program size. While their stories are complex and contain much that is particular to their specific situations, these congregations have helped me to understand what it might mean to "lay the foundation" for a difficult size transition. Here are the four preparatory tasks:

- Excavating the religious culture(s) of the congregation
- Building up a foundation for change using the congregation's own cultural materials
- Enriching the congregation's practices of democracy and discernment
- Assessing the congregation's progress on key dimensions of system change

When the groundwork has been laid in these four ways, "raising the roof"—that is, expanding institutional capacity in order to meet community opportunities and needs—becomes a realizable dream.

ASSUMPTIONS BEHIND THE RESEARCH

I began my research with one major assumption: namely, that a vital congregation searches for ways to reach and serve its surrounding population. Faith communities vary dramatically, of course, in the way they define the terms "reach," "serve" and "surrounding population." But for me, this is a foundational premise that branches into several corollaries.

First, I assume that growth in average sabbath attendance is one (but not the only) relevant measure of how adequately a congregation meets the needs of a growing community. (All of the study churches were located in growing towns, and the findings of this research are especially applicable to congregations facing the opportunities and challenges presented by population growth.)

Second, I assume that planting a new congregation is one effective way to reach a growing population; in that case, most of the growth in attendance takes place in the newly formed congregation. Changing size— "stepping up" decisively to a new level of institutional capacity—is another way to address the opportunity of population growth.

Third, I assume that size change, and especially the shift from pastoral to program size, is one of the most difficult transitions a congregation will ever navigate. Many aspects of the congregation's culture will have to change, and the church's enduring values will have to be expressed in new ways if the shift is to be made successfully.

Finally, I assume that size affects a congregation's public role. Community organizers have noted that larger congregations make better institutional partners for neighborhood improvement. Family- and pastoral-size churches have greater difficulty establishing human service programs, securing grants, forming community development corporations, and engaging in advocacy on behalf of vulnerable populations. Short-tenured and part-time pastors (common in churches with average attendance under 100) have less opportunity to develop community relationships or assume leadership positions within local boards and organizations.

Against this conceptual backdrop, let's look at what's involved in laying the groundwork for a pastoral-to-program size transition.

Preparatory Task 1:
Excavating the religious culture(s) of the congregation.

"Excavating the religious culture" sounds a bit like archaeology, doesn't it? A fine new resource called *How We Seek God Together: Exploring Worship Style*,[1] makes the case for viewing congregations as distinctive cultures. The authors define congregational cultures as "tool kits" made up of "stories, symbols, rituals, patterns of thought, world views with which people build a way of life." A congregation's culture (or cultures, since more than one distinctive culture may be manifest within a single congregation) can be explored by studying various cultural products such as worship, buildings or other physical artifacts, and mission activity in the local context.

Congregations with different cultures will define a term like "mission to the surrounding community" in different ways and will assign different religious meanings to an apparent opportunity for numerical growth. Using categories developed by church sociologists David Roozen, John McKinney, and Jackson Carroll (*Varieties of Religious Presence*, 1984[2]) we might characterize these different stances toward growth in broad terms.

For congregations with an *activist* religious culture, "God calls the *congregation* to speak out on issues and engage in corporate action, working for social change. . . ." Some activist churches see no need to be more than small cadres, more concerned about commitment than numbers; others seek to "build their base" of ministry (and consequently their numbers) through community organizing techniques.

The congregation with a *civic* culture promotes the public good through involvement with existing social and economic institutions. Internally, it "provides a forum in which social issues can be discussed and debated in a way that enables *individual* members to act responsibly as Christians. . . ." Civic churches tend to see themselves as part of the community fabric. They may view sabbath attendance as a minor measure as compared to the total number of people whose lives are touched by the ministries of the congregation and by the leavening influence of members scattered throughout the community. On the other hand, they may see building membership as a way to foster strength, openness, and diversity in their "little public." (I will elaborate on this last point in discussion of task 3.)

In a more *evangelistic* church culture, the "spirit of the Great Commission is at the center of congregational life"; congregants are "encouraged to witness to their faith, sharing the message of salvation with those outside the fellowship. . . ." Generally speaking, this religious tradition tends to value numerical growth as a sign that the Good News is being proclaimed effectively and that more people are being called into a life of discipleship. Numerical aspirations may be affected, however, by the degree of theological conformity required of new members.

Where the congregation sees itself primarily as *sanctuary*, members are called across the threshold into the congregation to experience divine transcendence over the trials of daily life. Christians are "expected to live in the world, accepting it as it is, and to uphold its laws; but they are to be 'not of this world' in their deepest loyalty which belongs only to God." Since weekly worship is a key spiritual discipline, growing attendance may be seen as an indicator that the congregation is engaged in effective spiritual formation of its members and inquirers. On the other hand, members may understand themselves as the "faithful remnant" and may expect few others to join them as they seek to enter through the narrow gate.

These four congregational cultures are "tool kits"[3] available to faith communities as they interpret shifts in their context and reimagine their own role in a changed environment. As you explore the culture of your faith community to lay the groundwork for a size transition, *How We Seek God Together* would be an excellent guide.

"Golden Rule" Christianity

No single set of categories can adequately describe all the nuances of congregational culture. Recent work by church sociologist Nancy Ammerman ("Spiritual Journeys in the American Mainstream," 1997[4]) offers another perspective on cultural differences that helped me to understand the seven churches in the study—as well as other congregations I have worked with on issues of numerical growth. Her analysis of extensive data from 23 churches (ranging from fundamentalist to Unitarian) revealed that about half the members overall shared an approach to religious life which she termed "Golden Rule" Christianity. This group was at least a substantial minority in even the most conservative congregations. Her appreciative portrayal of this cultural subgroup found within a wide spectrum of congregations may help you to interpret some of the growth-related conversations (and silences) in your own church.

Based on Ammerman's interviews, here are the kinds of phrases an imaginary group of Golden Rule Christians might use to describe their own spiritual path:

- The most important attributes of a Christian are caring for the needy and living one's Christian values every day.
- The most important task of the church is service to people in need.
- The Bible is important (even though few of us would call it the "inerrant" word of God).
- We are less concerned with answering life's great questions or developing a coherent theological system than with practices that cohere into something we can call a "good life."
- Our goal is neither to change another person's beliefs nor to change the whole political system. We would like the world to be a bit better for our having inhabited it.
- We have not given up on transcendence. The church's "sacred space" and the "sacred time" set aside for worship give many of us an opportunity to set our priorities in order, "feed the soul," and know that we have been in a presence greater than ourselves.

Most of the leaders I met in the course of my study expressed their faith using a Golden Rule idiom.[5]

If Ammerman's findings were shown to be representative of the general population, Golden Rule Christians would constitute the largest subset of church members in the United States. This could help explain why so many congregations have difficulty with the topic of numerical growth. Since Golden Rule Christians place a very high value on diversity and tolerance, they are not eager to challenge other people's religious beliefs or even, in most situations, to verbalize their own. One woman wrote me a letter explaining her feelings.

When I visited my grandparents in a small northern New York State town as a child of seven, I was reprimanded for going down by the railroad tracks with my friend to try to peek at those "strange people" who set up a tent to shout out the glory of God, sing boisterous hymns, and pray. . . . I don't think that was an unusual social stigma [i.e., any association with the religious culture of "holy rollers"]. Those of my age now . . . sometimes find it difficult to speak publicly about our faith and so we dedicate ourselves to the work of God and His Church. Doesn't the Church grow in spite of that type of faith?

Golden Rule Christians often exhibit an appealing modesty about their faith. Where this reticence is more intense, however, leaders may vehemently reject invitational outreach of any kind—even gentle communication with people who share (or who would readily appreciate) the congregation's approach to faith. This "allergic" reaction stands in tension with other core values of the Golden Rule path, such as offering a caring welcome for newcomers in the community. Though American culture in the 1950s operated like a dump truck, depositing people at the church's front door on Sunday morning so that mainline Protestant Christians could greet them, it now whisks prospective members off to the mall, the soccer field, the office, or the weekend getaway. Congregations that want to show "hospitality to the stranger" may need to build a more visible path (metaphorically and literally) to the doors of their spiritual home and provide more explanation about their faith tradition for those who do appear on the doorstep. But the "allergy" must be addressed in order for this kind of outreach to occur.

Across the sample of churches in the study, a number of specific issues emerged that related to the prominence of Golden Rule Christianity within each congregation's cultural make-up.

Intending growth. Congregations with a Golden Rule religious culture have an especially hard time forming, expressing, or endorsing an intention to grow numerically. Though all seven churches I studied were located in growing towns and were visited regularly by newcomers, many leaders disavowed any goal to increase church attendance. When my questions included the word *growth*, interviewees often prefaced their answers with a definition of the term that did not involve an increase in numbers. The subject seemed to provoke more than intellectual disagreement; in many conversations, the idea of *seeking growth explicitly* seemed to provoke slight twinges of discomfort, embarrassment, or distaste. Growth that "just happens" may be acceptable (and even a source of quiet satisfaction for some), but numerical growth intentionally sought seemed somehow to be regarded as an unworthy or shameful goal.

Only a few of the leaders I interviewed volunteered a clear moral or theological case for stepping up to the next size in order to make room for the people moving into their communities. In several of these congregations, leaders were surprised to see that their worship attendance had been stuck at a plateau for several years; tracking attendance trends was not part of their annual self-assessment.

Emphasis on children. With an apparent preponderance of Golden Rule Christians in the pews, what motivated the seven churches I studied to work at the tasks required for a size transition? By and large, concern for children and their parents was the biggest driving factor that pressed these congregations to expand their capacity even in the face of their reluctance to embrace numerical growth as an overall goal. "Religious and moral training for their children," says Ammerman, is "central in the circle of care" which defines a virtuous life for Golden Rule Christians. Within the seven churches in the "Raising the Roof" study, the Christian Education Committee typically played a key role in advocating for growth plans. Dynamic younger women often led the charge, and a few of these gifted leaders were later selected to serve as paid Christian education staff. In one of the churches, the elder generation expressed a high value on reaching children even before younger families had arrived in any number. Their long-range plan called bluntly for a transition to a new generation.

Children in worship. In the churches I studied, parents tended to want their children with them in worship at least part of the time each week. Children were typically attending the first part of the service and participating in communion when it was offered; one church went further by creating a new "early service" that involves children throughout. For some of the empty-nest and elder adults in these churches, weekly connection with youngsters in worship is a joy. For others of them (and even, perhaps, for some younger parents), this practice seems to collide with a longing for transcendence that they may have a hard time articulating. Ammerman's work sheds light on these particular yearnings. When she asked Golden Rule Christians about their experience of God, they often paused to search for words; some then responded that they felt "close to God in Sunday worship, especially in the music and in the opportunity for quiet reflection." Since Golden Rule members are less likely than others to attend programs designed for adult spiritual formation, especially in small group settings, many of these adults may cling to those familiar worship patterns as their one reliable touchstone with transcendence. This group may feel bereft of their particular experience of the holy when worship becomes more focused on children (one argument for multiple worship services).

Spiritual growth. By understanding and respecting the congregation's existing culture(s), leaders may develop the trust required to guide each cultural group—including the Golden Rule Christians—toward appropriate forms of spiritual growth. Religious cultures are dynamic; they evolve over time in response to external circumstances, internal needs, and the overtures of individual leaders. Ammerman challenges congregations to help Golden Rule adults and their children to develop a "sustained religious vocabulary" and to "[build] up the store of moral resources on which they can call for living the good and caring life to which they say they aspire." She concludes that the spiritual yearnings of the Golden Rule group are "as real as they are vague" and deserve respectful attention. The difficulty comes in persuading these members that they should actually show up for experiences that would deepen their spiritual life—especially small groups.

Among the seven churches I studied, one has a particularly effective strategy for adult education and spiritual development that seems to fulfill Ammerman's challenge with considerable success. Headed by a volunteer director (a retired private school dean), this program currently includes 20 different adult faith development offerings in the course of the year. Some are clergy-led, but most are not. Some last three or four sessions, while others are long-term study groups. The overall menu of choices addresses different styles of spirituality and learning.

It is probably not a coincidence that this same congregation scored especially high on two measures used in the study. The first instrument, developed in the course of this research, was the "System Change Index," which locates a congregation on nine dimensions of organizational transition required for healthy functioning at program size. (Factors in the index include congregational self-definition, pastoral role, size of staff, physical capacity, multi-cell functioning, delegation of planning tasks, aspirations to quality, infrastructure for member care, and conflict management. The full index appears in appendix E.) This particular church received the highest possible rating on almost every dimension. Its adult education strategy is just one example of its consistently "program" way of doing things—a variety of choices, high quality, and the deployment of staff (in this case a talented volunteer) to organize and direct a program delivered by many different leaders.

The second instrument was the "Margin in Life" inventory developed by nursing researcher Joanne Stevenson.[6] This inventory measures the impact of various factors, including religious practice, on a person's available reserves of energy, vitality, and resilience—a surplus she calls "margin." Adults draw upon these reserves when they embrace an opportunity for personal growth and learning, or when they confront a challenge such as illness, grief, or unexpected change. (See appendix C for a list of the factors measured by the "Margin in Life" instrument.) I administered this inventory to about 30 people in each church. Members of the particular congregation I have been describing seemed to have more "margin" in their daily lives; on average, these congregants scored highest among the seven congregations. While this finding caught my attention, the variations in average "margin" scores might well have arisen from demographic differences among towns and congregations rather than from differences in church structure or programming. But the specific contribution of religion to a member's "margin in life" was also the highest in this particular church. It seems reasonable to speculate that differences in scores on the religion factor might indicate a real difference in the impact each congregation makes on its members. Since my study involved such a small sample of congregations, this finding is only suggestive, but it reinforces a strong hunch. Remaining stuck in the transition zone seems to drain the margin (personal reserves of energy, vitality, and resilience) out of the lives of leaders and active members. Full transition to a "program" way of operating—combined with explicit attention to the spiritual development of adults—seems to allow the congregation to enhance people's "margin in life" more effectively.

Preparatory Task 2:
Constructing a foundation of authority for change using the congregation's own cultural materials.

When addressing growth opportunities, mainline Protestant congregations proceed from their own understandings of religious authority. Neither a Bible verse nor an admonition from the hierarchy will automatically answer to members' satisfaction the question: "Should we grow?" Resources from the church growth movement sometimes emphasize understandings of scriptural and pastoral authority that are foreign to, or constitute a minority position within, the religious culture of mainline Protestant churches. It seems that congregations with a liberal theology and a democratic polity need to "construct" the authority to change size from materials already available within their own religious culture. Some of these "materials" (potential cultural resources for authorizing a size change) may be well developed and ready at hand; the Golden Rule value on ministering to children and families is an example of a well-developed cultural resource for authorizing certain kinds of growth. Other cultural materials needed for constructing this foundation may currently lie out of reach, "buried" in one of two forms. They may lie underground as cultural "ore"—that is, latent source materials never uncovered or processed at all. (Each member's own faith story, for example, is a latent resource that, if brought to awareness and articulation, could provide people with the inner authority to invite others in authentic and respectful ways.) On the other hand, these cultural resources may lie beneath the surface in the form of "lost treasure"; that is, developed cultural materials discarded at a certain point in history or entombed in layers of cultural accretion. (An example of "lost treasure" might be the pre-Reformation spiritual traditions that shaped the devotion of Luther and Calvin, but were not carried forward into the next generation of Protestant religious life.) "Constructing" a foundation of authority for size change from materials that already belong to the religious culture may be an arduous task; nevertheless, this effort seems the surest way to build a solid basis for growth efforts.

For an individual leader, the issue of authority presents itself as a very practical question: "What right do I have to ask others in this church to change?" Or perhaps more pointedly, "What right do I have to ask this congregation to relinquish some of its familiar patterns and to adopt some new ways of being church?" Much has been written about the way an effective pastor brings personal authority (trustworthiness tested in the crucible of relationship) to his or her position of organizational power. Pastor and author James Adams[7] has captured this central challenge of clergy leadership in a single question: "Do I want to be in control or do I want to be taken seriously?" If the pastor is seen as disrespecting the congregation's culture (perhaps by disparaging the congregation's favorite hymns and instructing the musician to substitute "better" choices, for example), a power struggle will probably ensue. Members will feel that they have to defend the congregation's way of life against the intruder; in a process with many unconscious dimensions, the ruling spirit of the church's culture will "knight" certain people to do battle on its behalf. In contrast, when clergy proceed from an attitude of cross-cultural curiosity and respect, resistance to change is generally less severe. The way clergy exercise their religious authority does indeed have a major impact on the way a change is received.

However, when it comes to making a major shift with big implications for the church's culture—like the pastoral-to-program size transition—the authority of lay leaders becomes pivotal. By lay leaders, I mean not only the formal office holders, but also the informal opinion leaders within various constituencies. Even more than pastors, lay persons receive "permission" to lead to the extent that they are recognized (at least subconsciously) as carriers of the church's culture. This is particularly true in family- and pastoral-size congregations, where the dominant style is easily perceived and conserved. But even in larger congregations, where some cultural variety is likely to be acknowledged and negotiated, the most influential leaders are probably those who embody (or defer to) the dominant culture.

If a lay leader makes a bid to modify that culture (in response to new realities in the environment or new needs among members), he or she must demonstrate that the proposed change is "authorized" by values at the center of the culture itself. The change will only occur if it comes to be viewed as a "natural" step, a new chapter that emerges coherently from a unique congregational narrative. Except where there is a very long-tenured and well-loved pastor, lay leaders may actually have more authority than clergy to initiate cultural change, provided that they are astute interpreters of the congregation's story and have a clear "read" on the external environment. Perhaps you can see why I chose to place "excavating the religious culture(s) of the congregation" first on the list of preparatory tasks. A handful of well-trusted members can lead the way as the faith community retraces its roots and reinterprets its central values for a new day.

Let's turn now to some of the specific clues about sources of authority that surfaced in the study churches.

Biblical Authority

When asked directly, the pastor(s) and two lay leaders I interviewed in each church agreed rather strongly with the general assertion that growth is a biblical mandate. But in six of the seven churches, lay leaders almost never used biblical language or mentioned biblical themes when they talked about growth in their individual interviews or in the group storytelling. In only one church did a lay leader volunteer a statement that it was God's or Jesus' will that the church should grow at this time. Ammerman notes that a disinclination to invoke the Bible in an explicit or literalistic way does not mean that Golden Rule Christians find the Bible unimportant. In many cases, they simply have little practice putting into their own words the faith that underlies their everyday actions. Baby boomers with this faith style also tend to forget that they grew up in an environment saturated with religious stories and symbols. While they may be able to draw on this "spiritual capital" in times of need or decision, they may overlook the need to replenish that capital for themselves or to help succeeding generations understand the spiritual root system that generated the Golden Rule branch of religious life. (Paradoxically, notes Ammerman, they often undercut their own hopes for their children by neglecting the transmission of basic stories and precepts.) So, except for one church—whose culture includes both evangelical and Golden Rule components—the Bible was a tacit, but not an explicit, source of authority for size change in the congregations I studied.

Pastoral Authority

The lay leaders that I interviewed generally agreed with the assertion that their pastors "believe the church should grow at this time." But they often emphasized that the pastor's organizational role in promoting size change was low-key or behind the scenes—helping the congregation move toward its own decisions. Low-key did not mean insignificant; lay leaders noted the quiet power of their pastors' leadership. All seven clergy showed a marked preference for the "supporting" style of leadership (measured by the Blanchard LBA II inventory[8]) as opposed to a style of directing, coaching, or delegating. Several of the clergy manifested some ambivalence about seeking (or even tracking) growth in worship attendance. Despite their desire for growth in program scope, quality, and inclusiveness, this subset of the pastors seemed to mirror their congregations' hesitance to work explicitly toward increasing the average worship attendance (which I take to be one relevant measure of the congregation's caring for the spiritual needs of a growing town).

Golden Rule Authority

The Christian education leaders in each congregation who argued for expanded capacity—to serve children and their families better—were building a foundation for growth from materials already available in the church's religious culture. While any of the seven churches could probably serve as a case to illustrate this point, I will provide sample "cultural materials" from just one of the congregations.

- A report of the Christian Education Committee to the Annual Meeting in 1959 began with this statement about the committee's work: "We know that unless we are a teaching church, we are not a true church, so our greatest emphasis is on our Church School."
- The second sentence of the mission statement adopted by this church in 1996 reads: "Seeking God's guidance we aim, through the effective use of our resources, to meet present-day challenges, especially the fellowship, parenting, and Christian education needs of our congregation."
- Early in 1999, an "elder statesman" of this church looked back over the previous 10 years in the address he gave on Appreciation Sunday. "During the early and mid-eighties at virtually all Church Council Meetings, three real 'Needs' developed. The first and most serious need was the problem of not enough space or rooms for our Sunday School classes. [Our superintendent], who then, as now, primarily engineered this program, would plead, 'Where can I have my classes?' and indeed there was no good answer."

The power to authorize change does not lie in the documents themselves—current leaders may not recall or refer to these particular statements. The power resides in the underlying values of this congregation's religious culture, which are expressed in a variety of ways. Through the years, leaders in this church have shown confidence that they could legitimately ask their fellow members for change, sacrifice, and institutional expansion provided that the purpose was religious education for children.

Leaders in the seven churches have generally shown far less confidence about asking for change when the purpose is to increase (or, to put it more delicately, allow natural growth in) overall attendance. From a Golden Rule perspective, this is a tougher case to make. Nevertheless, one lay leader I interviewed did articulate an unusually passionate case for stepping up to the next size. He said this:

Ultimately, the message we kept trying to put out was Christian responsibility—not only to ourselves—responsibility to everyone who chooses to be part of us. If people want to worship here, we have a responsibility to furnish a second service, [second] Sunday school—[enough] programs to allow them to participate. This touches the consciences of people, and I have no conscience [i.e., qualms] about playing on people's consciences! Many are in between: "I want growth but . . ." There are things I'm not all that crazy about that are part of going from a small to a larger church— people I hardly ever see, not knowing too many on Sunday, though they know me. There is no free lunch.

This leader is one of the many early retirees who have moved to southeastern Massachusetts in the last decade. Based on his intense volunteer involvement with affordable housing advocacy, I would say that he personally manifests more of an "activist" than a "Golden Rule" religious culture. But by framing the question of growth in terms of "Christian responsibility," he was speaking a language that Golden Rule Christians would tend to take seriously. What most surprised his fellow members may have been his *passion* about issues of growth, but his quiet one-to-one approach helped others to grapple with his message.

Another respected leader of this congregation (a woman recovering from cancer who had been part of this church for more than 20 years) described the impact of his witness on her own and others' thinking. "[He provided a] tremendous push. He exemplifies what true Christianity is . . . very quiet [but still saying to us], 'This is what the Gospel is all about.' I thought, 'Oh, yeah! How could I have thought differently?'" As opposition to growth began to manifest itself, those who favored expansion began to take a more conscious stand. "[We asked ourselves,] 'What is our message?' Spread the word! Include children! Evangelistic work, open doors, invite, grow! Once I was 'there' I was happy—this is what I really believe. That was an 'Aha!' experience." In the middle of a tense and crucial meeting, she testified to the powerful support this congregation had provided during her cancer treatment, and she laid down a spiritual challenge: "I don't want this church divided." Others told her later that her speech had "turned them around." A large majority of those at the meeting endorsed the growth-related initiatives (including the two-service schedule already in place).

It appears that the newer leader—an assertive cultural "outsider" with activist inclinations—was able to awaken the conscience of Golden Rule members about their responsibility to make room for newcomers. Though he himself may not have used evangelical language, he seems to have stirred up in others some previously unexpressed convictions about spreading the Gospel. While this advocacy generated excitement (and support for longstanding staff efforts toward growth), it also increased the level of tension. Accomplishing the culture shift required for transition to program size has required several years of persistent effort and a cadre of leaders willing to pay the emotional cost (disapproval from some fellow members). Urgency about matters of growth is now becoming integrated into the congregation's self-understanding.

In faith traditions characterized to some significant degree by liberal theology and democratic polity, the authority to change size (and therefore to modify religious culture) must be "constructed" from materials at hand in the congregation's cultural "tool kit."[9] Lay leaders and clergy proceed most wisely when they help the congregation to explore in depth its own history and religious heritage. In this process, trusted members may be able to dig out a few durable, authoritative, and widely shared congregational values to serve as the footings for cultural change. Golden Rule Christians may then be more willing to accept the challenge and pay the price. Indeed, being ready to sacrifice in times of crisis is a Golden Rule value.

Preparatory Task 3:
Enriching the congregation's practices of democracy and discernment.

In nearly all the churches in this study, the religious value most frequently affirmed in leader interviews and group storytelling was democracy. This is partly attributable to the sample, which includes congregations that actually helped to invent the New England town meeting. However, because congregationalism has deeply influenced American religion as a whole, such adamantly democratic faith communities still have something to teach us. These churches function as "little publics," living and promoting an intense civic culture of their own. Urban sociologist Lowell Livezey[10] argues that this is one important way congregations contribute to the public good, and he commends proselytizing as an assertive way of being open and inclusive—active invitation builds the strength and diversity of the "little public." (This way of seeing evangelism may be helpful to mainline churches whose religious values have a strong civic dimension.)

In the pastoral-to-program size transition, it helps both to enrich the congregation's patterns of democratic participation and to develop (or reinforce) a complementary set of congregational practices for spiritual discernment.

Open Process

For the seven churches in the "Raising the Roof" study, democracy is a spiritual practice, and process questions carry moral weight. Change typically came about through repeated cycles of planning, decision making, and implementation. In each cycle, the congregation focused on extending its capacity in the way it believed most critical at that moment: expanding the building, adding staff, multiplying worship services, or raising capital funds. Sometimes the cycle began with work on an overall long-range plan; but sometimes proposals on a single topic (like parking) pressed the congregation toward a more comprehensive look at its life and its future. Whatever the sequence, the key to steady forward movement was an open and deliberate process, directed by respected laity with change management skills and supported by consistent clergy involvement (neither dominance nor complete delegation). Certain lay leaders functioned as "change champions" in each church—shepherding the growth project from one phase to the next and serving in a succession of growth-related leadership roles.

Moments of Truth

None of the churches made a one-time decision to "be program size." Yet each church came to at least one moment of truth: a situation or decision that became a crucial test of the congregation's willingness to change size. Pivotal events included:

- The vote to approve a building expansion or a purchase of land
- The addition of a second major Sunday service, a decision often intertwined with choices about the participation of children (In one case, a serious and painful conflict erupted with a motion to end the recently established second service. Charles Arn[11] has shown that this crisis is often delayed until the moment when the additional service overtakes the previous "main" service in attendance.)
- The debate over adding staff
- Turning people away on Easter morning (In one case, this experience galvanized the pastor and lay leaders to take action.)

Some congregations in the study experienced more than one of these moments of truth during their sojourn in the transition zone between sizes.

Effective Advocates

The need for good process is well understood by all seven churches in the study (even if they sometimes overlook a step or misjudge the degree of consensus). The need for effective advocacy may be a bit less obvious in these communities where "tolerance" and "diversity" are key words. Where no one expresses any passionate convictions, democratic processes have no fuel to drive them forward. While too much heat can burn out the engine, mainline Protestants rarely suffer from an excess of fervor about seizing opportunities for growth. Each of these churches had effective advocates who persistently made the case for expanding capacity, even in the face of some anxiety and resistance. Pastors and boards in each of the study churches provided room for these advocates to raise important issues. As a degree of tension developed, leaders channeled the resulting energy into some clear structure such as a formal planning process.

Healthy Norms for Conflict

Tension about growth stops generating useful energy when the system does not articulate and defend firm ground rules for disagreement. Two churches in the study did an exceptional job of addressing potentially volatile conflicts.

In the first case, the pastor and board referred a serious complaint about a staff member to a panel of leaders who conducted a formal inquiry—containing the dispute within firm boundaries and assuring the rest of the congregation that it was being handled responsibly. When the panel did not concur with the complaint, leaders conveyed to the aggrieved parties that the matter was closed; they did not allow the issue to fester.

In the second case, a member of the church's inner leadership circle took exception to a formal group decision and had trouble letting go of the issue even though his opinion clearly had not carried the day. In this congregation—whose dominant religious culture might be described as "liberal evangelical"—pastor and board spent time studying the standards for conflict found in Matthew 18 and communicated clearly to individual members that, after open discussion of viewpoints, the legitimate decisions of the congregation had to be respected. The pastors in both of these churches scored relatively well on both the flexibility and the effectiveness of their leadership style (as measured by the Blanchard LBA II instrument), and both tended to be proactive in the face of conflict.

In contrast, one church experienced an intense and painful growth-related conflict over the creation of a second worship service and church school program. (I have already described a bit of this fight in my discussion of Golden Rule authority.) In hindsight, the pastor and deacons believe that they overloaded the system by changing the basic order worship just before they went to the two-service schedule; this tension ultimately erupted in a bid to repeal the two-service decision. On the LBA II inventory, the pastor of this congregation rated somewhat lower on leadership flexibility. He frankly described himself to me as a person who had generally tended to avoid conflict prior to this experience. Although the system around him did not have enough compensating strengths in conflict management to prevent a painful win-lose resolution of the worship fight, the church was able to make a clear decision and move forward with its program—sometimes the most that can be achieved in particular circumstances. At the time of the interviewing, it did not appear to me that this congregation and its leaders had recovered their energy and confidence after this difficult experience. Since then, the two-service structure has taken hold and is operating well.

A congregation's ability to set healthy norms for handling disagreement is an important component of "readiness" for size transition. Two outstanding resources for this work are Denise Goodman's book, *Congregational Fitness*,[12] and Gil Rendle's *Behavioral Covenants in Congregations*.[13]

Democracy and Discernment

Author Charles Olsen and others have suggested that the great political and religious innovation of the 17th century—parliamentary governance—may need to be enriched in congregations with classic Christian practices of spiritual discernment. Just as individual Golden Rule Christians may benefit from small-group settings where they can tell and reflect upon their own faith story, whole congregations need practice in relating their local story to the "great stories" of faith, especially when important choices are being made. In an informal way, some of the study churches made use of a major anniversary celebration to retell the local story and to connect it with a core faith theme and a current sense of calling. One of the churches has a historical connection with the composer of the music for "Blest be the tie that binds" (the tune is named for this faith community); some leaders see that particular hymn as emblematic of the congregation's character. But with more explicit and consistent practices of spiritual discernment, these and other churches might add a deeper dimension to their decision making and gain greater confidence about articulating their special vocation.

Preparatory Task 4:
Locating the congregation on nine dimensions of system change.

Generally speaking, pastors and lay leaders underestimate the scope and extent of change that is required before a congregation hits its stride with a "program" way of operating. Without an accurate inventory of the degree and kind of change involved, leaders cannot solicit informed consent from the congregation. Even more fundamentally, leaders cannot properly assess their own commitment and capacity to see this transition through.

In the System Change Index, appendix E, I have identified nine dimensions of organizational change required in order to complete the transition from a "pastoral" to a "program" way of being church. I suggest that you try it out as a way of assessing where your congregation may be in its journey. Gary McIntosh provides another helpful way to measure size-related organizational change in his book, *One Size Doesn't Fit All.*[14]

WHERE TO GO FROM HERE

You have now completed the content sections of this book. I hope you have gained a deeper understanding of what may be involved in the transition from pastoral to program size. Now it is time to explore how other leaders in your congregation might engage in a season of learning, planning, and discernment around questions of size change. Chapter 4 provides detailed suggestions for structuring this time of learning.

CHAPTER 4

Five Steps
in Congregational Learning

Trainers have known for decades that leaders who attend a course—even an excellent one—rarely succeed in implementing everything they intend at the end of the course. As soon as they cross the boundary back into the organizational system, they are confronted with the system's powerful (and necessary) ability to resist any disruption of familiar patterns that might be caused by new ideas and behaviors. Leaders are quickly resocialized when they arrive "back home." The field of organization development was born as an attempt to bridge this gap—to move the learning process from outside the organization (and from a focus on changing one leader) to inside the organization (and to a focus on system learning and system change). Religious leaders who saw the potential of this approach created the field of congregation development and began designing ways for faith communities to learn and change from the inside out.

BEYOND INDIVIDUAL LEARNING

Though you may choose to read this book on your own as an individual learning experience (much like taking a course), the process described in this chapter presents you with an opportunity to bring this learning experience inside the congregation. Here are the five steps in this communal learning process:

1. Establish a covenant for learning.
2. Explore the unique character of this congregation.
3. Explore the unique character of our community context today.
4. Articulate our congregation's particular vocation within this context.
5. Adopt a plan for further learning and action.

By moving deliberately through these phases, you are creating a "holding environment" strong enough to contain anxiety and to engage leaders with the work of shared learning. The process is not meant to guarantee a decision to grow numerically or to adopt the practices of a program-size church; rather, the purpose is to help the congregation to face its situation honestly and to discern a shared direction.

OUTSIDE SUPPORT FOR THE LEARNING PROCESS

This chapter is addressed to an individual leader—ordained or lay—within the congregation who seeks to organize and guide a significant congregational learning process. While it is possible to initiate and lead such a process from the inside, the task will be far more difficult (and subject to more hazards) than if you have an appropriate outside partner supporting the process. Here are some options for finding that support.

Professional facilitator or consultant. You may want to partner with someone who is skilled in leading congregations through processes of planning and discernment. As a complete outsider, this person is the most likely to be seen as a neutral third party in the process.

Denominational staff person or trained volunteer. Through your denominational office, you may be able to identify someone who is able to work through this process with you. You will have to assess whether members will view this person as coming with an "agenda" different from the congregation's, and whether the person has the right skills to help.

Online support from the Alban Institute for a group of congregations from the same region moving through the same transition. Some of the materials in this book were originally developed for a pilot course conducted on an Internet learning site. If you (or your denominational office) can identify six to 12 congregations facing similar challenges, you may want to contact Alban's Consulting and Education department about options for online coaching through the learning process.

However you may proceed, you will want to observe some basic guidelines. Request references and speak with previous clients. Ask the potential partner to read the book before you finalize an agreement to work together, so that you can check their comfort with the material. Identify which parts of the process this person will assist with—I would especially suggest involving such a partner in the covenant meeting with the board, the first meeting of the learning team, the learning event for a wider circle of leaders, and the presentation of the team's work to the board at the end of the process.

CIRCLES OF INVOLVEMENT

As you move through these five steps, you will be working with three "circles" of system involvement in the learning process. The first circle is a learning team you will recruit to guide the work. The second circle around the learning team includes your primary governing board. The third circle around the team and the board is a wider group of de facto congregational leaders.

Working back and forth across the circles, the team will practice articulating and applying the concepts. They will gather vital information about the reactions and perspectives of other leaders in your system. And they will build a critical mass of members who can understand and support the recommendations the team will bring forward at the end of the process for further congregational learning and action (see figure 5).

You may have noticed that the "whole congregation" is not in the picture. In midsize and larger churches, learning and change are always mediated through circles of formal and informal leadership. Becoming conscious of how those circles operate—and helping them to perform their natural function within the larger body of the congregation—will be part of your work. Let me describe who is involved in each circle.

The learning team. This group leads the learning process. Its members will:

- Master size transition concepts and consider how they may apply to your particular congregation.
- Gather and evaluate the required information about your congregation.
- Plan and implement learning activities with the board and the wider circle of leaders.
- Lend their voices and perspectives to the task of communicating new concepts to others.
- Draft a statement of vocation and a proposed plan based on this cycle of learning.

Figure 5
Circles of Involvement

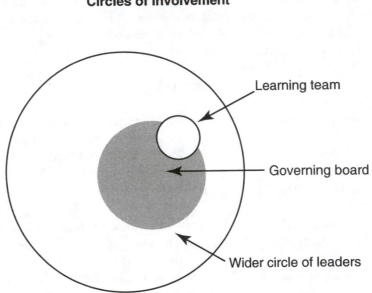

Learning team

Governing board

Wider circle of leaders

I recommend that you form a team of five to seven people, including the (senior) pastor. This team will meet regularly over a period of about eight months. In addition, members should plan to be present for learning conversations with the board and with the wider leadership circle.

The governing board. For the purposes of this course, "governing board" means a body (usually elected) that exercises general governance or oversight responsibilities in the congregation. It may be called a session, vestry, parish council, executive board, prudential committee, board of trustees, or steering committee. Some congregations have multiple boards and councils. In that case, you may either select the one that has the most general oversight role, or invite several different oversight bodies to join together for the "board learning" conversations. If, for example, financial and spiritual oversight are divided between trustees and deacons, try to involve them both. Many boards see their main work as approving and rejecting proposals; part of your task is to invite them (at least for a few short periods of time over eight months) to adopt a different stance—to see themselves as a learning community. This will only happen if there is a climate of trust within the board.

Wider circle of leaders. Every congregation has a de facto leadership circle. These are people to whom the rest of the members look when they are wondering whether to support or resist a project. Some of them are in visible, official leadership roles on boards, committees, and task teams. Others are informal leaders—people whose opinions others take seriously when they are deciding about an important issue.

LEARNING GOALS

The expected outcomes of this five-step process for team members, board, and wider circle of leaders include:

- Shared concepts
  - Size categories and characteristics
  - Plateau zones between sizes
  - Change dynamics involved in the pastoral-to-program transition
- Historical and spiritual perspective on your congregation's community setting, its sense of distinctive "calling," and its attitudes about size
- A proposed statement of the congregation's calling today
- A proposal to the board outlining next steps in learning, decision, or implementation regarding a size change

Among these potential outcomes, the single most important may be the development of a widely shared sense of the congregation's calling within its present context.

PREPARATORY TASKS

Before you begin to structure the learning process, you have some preparation to do. First, take a moment to recheck the fit between your congregation and the type of church for which this particular process was designed (see figure 6).

Figure 6
Descriptors of Churches That Will Benefit from This Process

Church Descriptors	Yes, we fit	We only fit partly	No, we don't fit	Don't know
Average year-round attendance (all Sunday* services, all ages) has hit a plateau somewhere between 150 and 250 (i.e., between "pastoral" and "program" size).				
The congregation is located in a context favorable to numerical growth. Likely indicators might be continuing population growth in the surrounding community and/or steady increases in total church membership while attendance remains stuck at a constant level				
The congregation regularly attracts first-time visitors to Sunday* worship.				
Both the pastor and lay opinion leaders believe that the congregation may be called to "step up" to the next size, and wish to engage in discernment and planning.				
Basic trust exists among pastor, lay leadership, and congregation.				
A small team of leaders can be found with the skills and motivation to guide others through a learning experience.				

*Congregations with Saturday evening or Sunday evening alternatives to Sunday morning worship should include unduplicated attendance at these services in their count. Children in education or nursery programs who do not participate in the main worship service should still be counted.

To the extent that your congregation does not fit this profile, you will need to modify your goals and adapt your approach.

Next, consider your role. If you are the sole or senior pastor, your role will probably allow you to initiate discussion—starting with a few of your key lay leaders—about launching a formal learning process. If you are a lay leader (perhaps a moderator, board chair, or committee head) you will want to involve your pastor in this project right from the beginning, including discussion of the "church descriptors" in the above chart.

Now, make an assessment the trust level within your governing board. Ask yourself:

- Do people look relaxed at the meetings?
- Do they greet each other warmly and take time to catch up with each other personally?
- Do people readily speak up, ask for clarification, and offer thoughts about agenda and procedure?
- Does everyone participate in the conversation?
- Are people at ease disagreeing with opinions that have been offered?
- Do people keep comments focused on issues and avoid personal attacks?
- Would you be eager to return for the next meeting if you were a board member?

To the extent that you answer yes to these questions, you probably have the supportive climate you need to form learning agreements with the board fairly quickly. To the extent that your answer is no, you will have to allow more time for discussion in order to develop these agreements—time to answer questions, provide background about your own motivations, and solict members' concerns about participating. You are not "losing time" if you slow down to bring the board along with you in the learning.

Finally, after you have finished reading this chapter, prepare an overview of the whole process you are asking the board to authorize and support. Figure 7 gives you a suggested outline to help you create that overview, but you will probably make adjustments to fit your situation.

Figure 7
Steps and Tasks in the Process

Time	Step	Tasks	T	B	W
First 2 months	1. Covenant for learning	a. Authorize whole learning process; obtain commitment of board to participate and to receive results.		✓	
		b. Select and recruit learning team.		✓	
		c. Hold first meeting of learning team.	✓		
		d. Establish dates for all key events.	✓	✓	
		e. Conduct first learning session with board.	✓	✓	
Months 3 and 4	2. Explore character of the congregation	a. Create 30-year attendance chart and pin map.	✓		
		b. Reflect on history of connection between congregation and context (larger learning event).	✓	✓	✓
		c. Summarize learnings about faith and context.	✓		
		d. Assess and summarize barriers to growth.	✓		
		e. Foster conversation about findings to date.	✓	✓	✓
Month 5	3. Explore character of the community context today	a. Identify trends in the wider culture.	✓		
		b. Check perceptions of community context using a demographic profile.	✓		
		c. Check perceptions using community leader interviews.	✓		
		d. Foster conversation about findings to date.	✓	✓	✓
Months 6 and 7	4. Articulate vocation	a. Prepare draft statement of the congregation's calling today.	✓		
		b. Prepare draft plan for further learning and action.	✓		
		c. Foster conversation about findings to date	✓	✓	✓
Month 8	5. Adopt plan	a. Bring revised statement of vocation and draft plan to board for formal action.	✓	✓	

T = Learning team involved in this task
B = Board and pastor involved in this task
W = Wider circle of leaders involved in this task

PRACTICES OF DISCERNMENT

While many other aspects of a congregation's life can be "planned" in more or less conventional ways, a calling must be discerned. *Discernment* may be understood as a "prayerful, informed, and intentional attempt . . . to get in touch with God's Spirit at work in a situation and to develop a sense of the direction in which the Spirit is leading." I have drawn this definition from a fine little book called *Grounded in God*;[1] if you are not familiar with tools for group discernment that fit your own tradition, you may want to refer to *Grounded in God* for background and practical suggestions.[2] In appendix F, I have provided some biblical reflections that might be used during team meetings, board learning conversations, or the event for a wider circle of leaders.

I believe that the Spirit is at work in your local community (and mine) drawing hearts deeper into the holy, deeper into the heart of God. We do not create or manage this sacred attraction, but we—as individuals and as congregations—are invited to cooperate with it. I believe that congregations are invited to play a unique and irreplaceable role in the Spirit's work of drawing hearts to their true home. I believe that each congregation has a responsibility for the spiritual growth of its current members, and an equal responsibility to offer a trustworthy spiritual path to those who are searching for—or estranged from—the sacred center of their lives. This is a bit of my own vocabulary of faith. Eight months from now, I hope you have found your own.

ADAPTING THE PROCESS

In the sections that follow, I suggest specific tasks for implementing each step in the process. These ideas are intended as a starting point in your planning; they reflect my own learning as I have worked with congregations in this particular transition. In many cases, you will have a good reason to frame the tasks differently. Always use your own best judgment about how the other leaders in your congregation learn best and about what kinds of processes they will accept.

Step 1:
Establish a Covenant for Learning.

The groundwork laid in the first few months will have a profound effect on the rest of the process. Take time to clarify the whole process in your own mind, and to build a shared understanding of what will happen.

Task 1a: Seek authorization for the learning process; obtain board commitment to participate and to receive the results.

In this transitional stage, it is crucial to affirm the role of the board and to build the board's capacity for learning and discernment. By starting with the board—before creating a learning team—you signal that you take their role seriously. Here are some suggestions.

Preparatory reading. Encourage board members to do some preparatory reading before you propose a more extended learning process. Chapter 1 and the beginning of chapter 4 (up through the grid of steps and tasks on page 62) would be especially helpful. Selected segments of the video *What Size Should We Be?*[3] may be used, if a visual medium is desired, to familiarize your board with the four size categories and with the concept of a size plateau. (The video offers a slightly different numerical range for program size; let the board know that the book you are reading now reflects my most current thinking and provides the definitions that you will be using in the rest of the process.)

Assess readiness with church descriptors. Duplicate the chart of "church descriptors" from earlier in this chapter (page 60) for each member of the board. At the beginning of your discussion with them about whether to undertake this extended learning process, ask each member to rate the items individually. Collect the sheets and collate the results on a chart pad as a way of launching the discussion.

Introduce learning process. Using the beginning of this chapter (pages 55-59) as your guide, present:

- the five steps (just the one-line headings)
- the circles of involvement
- the tasks of the learning team
- the learning goals

Once people are clear about those elements, share the chart of steps and tasks on page 62.

Clarify board commitment. Specify what you are asking of the board. Their commitment includes:

- Formal endorsement of the whole learning process
- Exploring size transition issues through personal reading, thought, and prayer
- Making this time of learning a priority among activities of the congregation
- Assigning excellent leaders to the learning team
- Spending regular or special board meeting time discussing the concepts and findings that the team brings forward
- Participating fully in the event(s) for a wider circle of leaders
- Anticipating some congregational anxiety about the outcome of the process
- Sticking to the established steps and avoiding premature decisions

Set date for board learning session. Establish the date for an initial learning session between the team and the board—one full hour of conversation scheduled within the next four to eight weeks. Ask board members to review chapter 1 and to read chapter 2 in preparation for this session.

Task 1b: Select and recruit a learning team to lead the process.

In chapter 3, I noted that congregations moving well through the pastoral-to-program size transition tend to delegate certain aspects of the work to leaders with particular gifts. That's what your board will be doing as it authorizes a learning team to lead this process. Since the team is charged to involve other leaders in specific ways, it should be relatively small—a size that promotes easy teamwork and creative thinking.

Criteria. Here are some guidelines for team selection.[4]

- Five to seven persons, including the (senior) pastor
- People who can listen openly for where God is calling this congregation next

- People familiar with the satisfactions and pinches experienced by members, newcomers, and visitors in your church today
- People who understand the political realities of your church
- People who work well with the pastor
- People who have a "voice" back in the congregation and are listened to when they speak
- People who can stay calm and work creatively in the face of some congregational anxiety

Since you are trying to fit the right gifts to the task, it is also helpful to identify characteristics that will not contribute to the effectiveness of this particular team. It is best not to invite:

- People unwilling to learn new things and think new thoughts
- People unable to consider potential consequences
- People unwilling to change themselves or their church to accommodate the needs of other people
- People with "axes to grind" about their church or their pastor
- People too busy to be effective
- People who overreact to other people's anxieties

Selection process. Involve the board in selecting the team. Here is one possible process that can help the board to focus on giftedness for this work.

- Review the role of the team, using the description on page 57-59.
- Share the above criteria for team members (both lists) with the board, then invite them to add other criteria of their own.
- Distribute blank index cards and ask each member to write on a card the names of three people who—in their estimation—fit the first list and don't fit the second. (People may nominate themselves if they feel they fit the criteria.)
- Collect the cards, then take a coffee break.
- During the break, sit with a trusted member of the board and with the pastor to collate the information from the cards and come up with a slate of six people to invite, in addition to the pastor. (Often, you will simply take the six names mentioned most often. If that produces a group that is obviously unbalanced—all women or retirees, for example—select someone a bit farther down the list to make up your slate of six.)
- Bring the slate back for board endorsement.

Recruitment. When you invite potential team members to participate, provide each with the list of team responsibilities (pages 57-59) and with a copy of this book. Ask them to read chapter 1 and the beginning of chapter 4 (up through the chart of steps and tasks on page 62) before they make a final commitment to participate, so that they can verify that they have the time and inclination to do this substantial piece of work. Congregations that use this method to identify candidates for learning and planning teams seem get mostly "yes" responses from those they invite.

Task 1c: Conduct the first meeting of the learning team.

Allow about two-and-a-half hours for the meeting, including a break. Here are some suggestions for this meeting.

Gather. It is important to begin to build a climate of discernment and trust right from the beginning.

- Begin with a time of prayer, quiet reflection, or devotional reading. You may want to use one of the biblical reflections from appendix F.
- Allow members a few minutes each to introduce themselves, to share their reasons for saying yes to serving on this team, and to express any questions or concerns.

Establish a framework. Using the beginning of this chapter (pages 55–62) as your guide, present for review:

- The five steps (just the one-line headings)
- The circles of involvement
- The learning goals
- The chart of church descriptors

Involve the team in assessing congregational readiness.

- On the chart of church descriptors, ask members of the learning team to check off their impressions, just as you did with the board.
- Discuss any differences between the team's assessment and the assessment made by the board.

Explore the charge to this team.

• Review the criteria employed by the board in selection of the team (both lists from pages 65 and 66). This helps team members to consider the behaviors and attitudes that will help and hinder the team's work.
• Review the tasks of the learning team (from pages 57-59).

Clarify key concepts.

• Referring to figure 1 (page 6), describe the four size categories.
• Referring to figure 2 (page 11), review the concept of a plateau zone between sizes.
• Invite questions and discussion.

Break.

Share details of learning process.

• Review with the team the overview of the whole process that you presented to the board (based on the chart on page 62.)
• Note the date the board has set for step 1e (an initial learning session between board and team).

Set date for larger learning event. Set a tentative date for gathering your wider circle of leaders about two months from now. This gathering will require about three hours, including a break. Take a few moments now to review the process for this event (pages 80-83) to get a feel for what it will require from you and from the participants.

Identify people to invite. Begin developing a list of your "wider circle of leaders." Congregations in the plateau zone between pastoral and program size will typically have 30 to 50 people who fill formal and informal leadership roles. One of your most crucial tasks is to become clear about who these people are and how they influence others in the congregation. I regard personal influence as a gift, given for service to God and community. Listing those with particular influence is not meant to keep others out; when in doubt, include.

- You may wish to use an exercise devised by Alban senior consultant Roy Oswald, described in figure 8. You will need a separate sheet of paper divided into the following four columns.

Figure 8
Power Analysis Chart

Reputational Power	Coalitional Power	Communicational Power	Official Power

POWER ANALYSIS OF A CONGREGATION
Roy M. Oswald

Under Official Power, list all those persons who hold elected offices in the parish. For a large parish, limit this list to those in official decision-making positions.

Under Reputational Power, list that handful of people who have the respect of most persons in the community [ie, the congregation]. These people have a certain charisma about them. When tough decisions get made in the parish, people usually look sideways to see where these people stand on the issues.

Under Coalitional Power, first list all the formal and informal subgroups that exist in the parish. This should include every group from the choir to the church bowling league. Include also the informal groups that cluster together on Sunday mornings. Also list the key individuals within each of these subgroups—those one or two individuals who are ringleaders. Depending on how the ringleaders feel about you or an issue, these subgroups can be mobilized either for or against you.

Under Communicational Power, list the informal communication networks within the parish. Try to answer the question, "Who has whose ear?" Who calls whom when there is some news to share? Include here people who spend a lot of time around the church building (e.g., church secretary, janitors, retired workers, etc.). These people usually have a lot of information about the activities of the parish. Those people who know "what's going on" are far more powerful than those who are in the dark. In this column, list those people who always seem to be in the know.

You now have people listed under four categories who represent power currencies within a parish. Go over all four lists and note names that appear on more than one list. Those names that appear on two or more lists are the most powerful people in the parish. Write these power people's names on a special list. Spend a few minutes with each name and rate your credibility with each person:

1   2   3   4   5   6
Low Credibility   High Credibility

This rating may give you some idea where you need to do some work if certain issues are to be resolved. You may decide you need to spend some time with certain folks in order to build a power base for yourself within the parish.

You may also want to rate each of these people with regard to their positions on specific issues. For example, if you are up against a key vote at a congregational meeting, rate each person's views on that issue:

1	2	3	4	5	6
Negative				Highly Supportive	

If the majority of these key persons are for the proposal, you can be fairly sure it will pass. To make sure, you may decide to visit a few key leaders who seem to be sitting on the fence. We do not recommend taking an issue to the parish as a whole unless you are fairly certain it will pass. When key issues fail to pass, your credibility and reputation may be diminished. This makes you less powerful when other issues arise.

Power dynamics affect each local parish. Most congregational members have their own assessment of power and control issues within their parishes. This is a given. So deciding whether or not you will undertake a power analysis of the parish is not the issue. At issue is whether you will be good at the process and disciplined in your approach or ignore the issues and handle power poorly. You may have to confront your personal feelings of comfort or discomfort with the use of power and clarify your theology of power.

From New Beginnings: A Pastorate Start-Up Workbook *(Bethesda, Md.: The Alban Institute, 1989). Used by permission.*

Plan to recruit. Now that you have a better idea of the target list for the larger learning event, divide up the task of inviting among members of the learning team. Remember that a personal conversation is always the best way to make an invitation; least effective is a general announcement in the newsletter or in church—though such announcements are useful to supplement individual invitations and to keep everyone in the congregation aware of what's going on. View the larger learning event as an open meeting for which you have done some careful recruitment.

Prepare to ask. Here are some points you will want to make when you recruit.

- Our congregation is experiencing a wonderful time of opportunity and also some growing pains.
- The board has asked us to think about our congregation's distinctive role and calling in this community today.
- You are a key person in this church, and we need your input.
- On (date), we are going to look at both our heritage and our present challenge. We'd like you to be there because you have a valuable perspective on things that no one else can bring.
- Can I sign you up to be there?

Some congregations have success with taking reservations for a "catered" meal (even if that's a couple of buckets of chicken from a fast-food restaurant). Such arrangements communicate a sense of importance about the gathering. Participants are less likely to cancel if they have made a definite reservation with you.

Plan future meetings of learning team. Set dates for the second and third meetings of the learning team. At the second meeting you will:

- Prepare for your first learning conversation with the board (guidelines on pages 74-76).
- Assign data gathering tasks (30-year attendance chart and pin-map of households—see instructions on pages 78-80).
- Check how recruitment is going for the larger learning event.
- Set an additional meeting date. (I suggest that you always have at least two future dates on your team calendar—that way, if one session has to be cancelled, there is always another meeting time planned.)
  At the third meeting, you will:

- Prepare for the larger learning event (see guidelines on pages 80-83).
- Study results of data-gathering tasks.
- Set an additional team meeting date.

As the learning team prepares for meetings with board and the wider circle of leaders, it will help to adopt the attitude of anthropologists visiting an unknown culture—suspending as far as possible your assumptions about what others think and how they will react. During these conversations with other groups, make sure one or two members of the team are writing down (perhaps on a chart pad) exact words and phrases offered by participants. Ask participants to tell you more about the thoughts and feelings behind their comments. Notice which contributions you find most surprising, puzzling, or distressing—the team will probably learn the most from the parts of the conversation that set you "off balance" in some way.

Task 1d: Establish dates for all key events.

In the learning session you are about to conduct with the board, you will want to offer them a calendar for the whole process. My suggested chart doesn't take into account holiday seasons, blizzards, or summer vacations—the team will tailor that suggested sequence to the realities of life. Your calendar should now include:

- Dates for several team meetings.
- Date for at least two major conversations (an hour each) with the board: one is the initial learning session that should be coming up quite soon; the other should occur near the end of step 4, to discuss questions of calling and next steps. I strongly recommend that you separate this discussion from formal action (step 5) so that the conversation is not reduced to group editing of a document. This type of discussion can diminish both the quality of conversation and the substance of the resulting statement.
- Date(s) to meet with the wider circle of leaders (either "mini-retreat" of about three hours, or two separate sessions), which you are asking the board to attend.
- A 24-hour learning team retreat, at the beginning of step 4. This type of spiritual and creative work requires a conducive atmosphere and a leisurely pace. If possible, get away from your church site and stay overnight in a quiet setting.

- A target date for adoption of a plan for further learning and action. It is wise to make this a tentative date, so that you are not rushed by an artificial deadline if you are not ready. As you shape your calendar, don't let a fixed date—like an annual meeting, for example—force you to finalize something you aren't confident about. You can always bring your "learnings to date" to such a gathering for small-group discussion—a process that generates lots of useful response without inviting the kinds of annual meeting behavior most of us dread (such as grammar debates, parliamentary maneuvers, and long speeches from the same few people.)

Task 1e: Conduct initial learning session with the board.

Introduction (about 10 minutes)

- Introduce the learning team.
- Refer to the Learning Goals for the whole process (page 59). Note that during this hour the board will be focusing on the first goal.
- Brief silent reflection:

> Write down the name of the first congregation that made a strong positive impression on you. It might be a church you attended as a child; a congregation you encountered as a teenager; or a congregation you discovered as an adult. Note a few things that made this congregation significant for you.

- Brief sharing with one other person, based on the silent reflection. (One minute per person—it's actually possible to say quite a bit in one minute.)

Past experience with four size categories (10 to 15 minutes)

- Write the names of the four sizes on a chart pad.
- One at a time, read aloud the descriptions of the four sizes from the first section of chapter 1. (Or, use the video segment labeled "1a" from

What Size Should We Be? Note that the numbers for program size are slightly different in the video from those in chapter 1. To avoid confusion, I suggest that you put the numerical ranges from chapter 1 on the chart pad next to the size names.)

- As you read the size descriptions, pause after each and ask people to raise their hands if that description fits the congregation they just identified in the reflection. (If you are using the video, play the whole segment first, then ask people to raise their hands for each of the four categories.)
- Note on the chart pad the number of people who raised their hands for each category.

Discussion (10 minutes)

- Ask: "Which category does our congregation most resemble today? Why?"
- Ask: "How do our own memories of church in the past affect our feelings about size change?"

The concept of a plateau zone

- From chapter 1, read aloud the first paragraph of the section entitled "The Pastoral-to-Program Plateau Zone" (pages 10 and 11, including the three examples of ambivalence). (Or you can show segment "1b" of the video at this point.)
- Ask people to look at the the the sample attendance chart I provided in that paragraph. (It will help if you have prepared in advance a sketch or enlarged photocopy of that plateau zone graph on the top half of your easel pad, so that you can direct the group's attention to it now.) Ask members to discuss why the church in the example might have plateaued.
- On the bottom half of the chart pad, point to a similar chart you have prepared with no attendance data filled in. Ask board members to discuss what they think the chart will look like, once your learning team has gathered your own church's attendance data.
- Ask the board members: "Besides numerical data, what other clues do you see that indicate we might be stuck in a plateau zone?" Write down on the chart pad as best you can the key words and phrases board members contribute.

Closing (about 5 minutes)

- Thank the board for their participation.
- Confirm the date for the gathering of your wider circle of leaders. Let them know that you will be bringing a 30-year attendance chart to that event, which board members can compare with the impressions they shared tonight.
- Pray together for guidance and discernment in the next steps of the process.

STEP 2:

EXPLORE THE DISTINCTIVE CHARACTER OF YOUR CONGREGATION.

The more a congregation comes to understand its own uniqueness, the better equipped it will be to hear God's call and to "dance" with its context. Jean Morris Trumbauer, who has written about member ministry development, makes this observation about the relationship between self-understanding and discernment of one's call:

> Many people worry about God's will regarding decisions they are about to make. Elizabeth O'Connor, popular author from the Church of the Saviour in Washington, D.C., reminds us that God's will is connected with the gifts we are given: "Our obedience and surrender to God are in large part our obedience and surrender to our gifts."[5]

We can say the same thing about a church—a still small voice is calling the congregation from deep within, from the heart of its very particular (even peculiar) character and its unique constellation of gifts.

When I say "gifts," I include the predictable items that might be listed in a parish profile for a clergy search: "historic building," "diverse and talented membership," "good choir." But to hear the whisper of a unique call—deeply rooted in the past and deeply relevant to today's context—leaders need to find a much more subtle and idiosyncratic vocabulary of congregational giftedness. I remember working with a very small congregation, located almost on the Canadian border. Most of the congregation's active adults were in the room, and each person had just shared a few words about their favorite hymn. One man said that he especially liked "Be thou my vision" (a well-known hymn from Irish origins). He pointed out that it wasn't just the hymn that moved him—what really made an impression was hearing it sung in Van Morrison's gritty voice. "That song is kind of like us," he said. "We're cranky and cantankerous, but still there's this longing for God." My eyes still fill up with tears when I remember his words. He had said something profoundly true about his little church—a far more telling portrait than any conventional profile could ever provide.

In this section, I am going to suggest several ways to develop a description of the congregation's character and situation, including an exercise for exploring call through the history of congregation and community. But the exercises I am offering are just a beginning point. It is my hope that you will do much more of this kind of exploration—before, during, and after this eight-month study. In particular, I hope you will review two outstanding resources, and perhaps select one to augment and enrich the process I am suggesting here.

First, I would call your attention again to a resource mentioned in chapter 3, the package (book and video) called *How We Seek God Together: Exploring Worship Style*.[6] This material can help you to perceive the distinctive character of your congregation through the lens of worship style. The video compares the style of three congregations within a similar denominational tradition; closely coordinated with the taped vignettes, the book provides concepts and exercises that will help leaders to notice and name the more subtle markers of a congregation's unique personality. An adult study series using this resource would provide excellent preparation for the process presented in this chapter.

Second, I would encourage you to explore Celia Allison Hahn's book, *Uncovering Your Church's Hidden Spirit*.[7] Hahn set out to learn about the distinctive spirituality of four congregations, using individual interviews as the primary method. After defining congregational spirituality in part I of her book, she goes on in part II to describe the process by which four congregations tried to answer the questions, "Who are we called to be?" and "Where are we called to go?" In part III, she offers learnings from the research that could help congregations undertake this kind of exploration themselves.

One of the most fascinating products of her research is a method for discovering who the real "spiritual leaders" are in your congregation. Hahn needed this information in order to develop her list of people to be interviewed, but this process of identification became, in itself, a powerful intervention into the life of the congregation. While an attempt to name people as "spiritual leaders" could be rather elitist, I think you will see from her comments that this was quite the reverse—she listened very carefully to the "mind of the congregation":

> To find the laypeople to interview, we created a questionnaire titled "Who should be interviewed for this project? We want your nominations," which every church put in its worship bulletin.
>
> Patrick Henry, of the Institute for Ecumenical and Cultural Research in Collegeville, Minnesota, made the suggestion early: "One of the most intriguing ways to go about it would be to ask them to list three or four people they think you should interview and then say why. Spiritual maturity becomes something embodied. Talk to the few who are on everybody's list." I agreed instantly. A questionnaire to the congregation would give us a *congregational* slant on perceptions about spirituality.
>
> I moved ahead with this plan, circulated a draft of possible questions to the advisory committee for feedback, and designed a church-bulletin-sized questionnaire. Clergy were very willing to put it in the Sunday bulletin, collect responses, and adjust the list of most-frequently-named "sages" so that it didn't include all men, or all newcomers, for example, but was reasonably balanced. . . . The project evaluation indicates how empowering this method was for many of those chosen.[8]

Because this is a very sensitive area of life for congregations and individuals, I would encourage you to use this method only after you have studied Hahn's book.

Having identified some rather lofty aims for this part of the process, I am going to encourage you to begin with "brass tacks"—figuratively and literally. The first steps involve gathering attendance data and creating a pin-map of your congregation's households.

Task 2a: Create a 30-year attendance chart and a pin-map

At the second meeting of the learning team, you will want to assign subgroups that will pursue each of these tasks and bring back the results the next time the team gathers.

Attendance chart. Using figure 2 (page 11) as a model, create a 30-year *11* attendance chart. Here are some guidelines:

- Calculate average attendance for each of the last 10 years. For the previous 20 years, plot data for selected years at three- or five-year intervals.
- For each year you are going to plot, gather attendance figures for all 52 Sundays, including Easter. If your primary Christmas service happens to fall on Saturday evening or Sunday in a given year, eliminate that Sunday and count twice the attendance for the following Sunday.
- Congregations with Saturday evening or Sunday evening alternatives to Sunday morning worship should include unduplicated attendance at these services in their weekly count. In the following directions, interpret "Sunday" to include these other sabbath services as well.
- For each Sunday, count the total number of people of any age who attended or who served as a leader in one or more of the following: sabbath worship services; church school for children, youth, or adults; nursery care during worship. Count each person only once for a given weekend. Total all 52 weeks and divide by 52 to compute an average attendance for that year.
- If your church has not kept attendance records for church school children but has kept registration records, use a percentage to estimate attendance from registration. (I might use a figure of 50 percent, to account for variations in weekly attendance and for the fact that classes typically run for nine months rather than 12.)
- Review the discussion in chapter 2, barrier 2, about the dynamics that occur when you begin to discuss attendance figures. These dynamics will probably occur in the team, and they will probably emerge again every time you present the data to a new group. Keep pressing each group to come to consensus on the most reasonable estimate.

Pin map. Locate each of the congregation's households on a large map attached to foam-core mounting board. Here are some guidelines:

- Look through your congregation's list to determine how wide a geographical area the map needs to cover. Choose a large enough map to show the homes of about 95 percent of your active members.
- You will need map pins in three colors. Use a bright color to designate households of your most recent members and attenders—those who

have started participating within the last three or five years, for example. These pins will tell you whom the congregation is currently attracting. Use a second color to designate the other active households in your congregation. Use a third color to designate inactive households, or people whose membership is an expression of loyalty to the congregation they used to attend.

• Some congregations involve members in plotting their own households on the map—an activity that can create curiosity and foster conversation throughout the congregation. If you choose to do this, you will have to make sure that the map is tended (say, during coffee hour) so that each household can be checked off the list as its location is plotted.

Task 2b: Engage your "wider circle of leaders" in historical reflection on the connection between congregation and context (larger learning event).

You will need about three hours for this conversation; or, you may want to schedule two separate gatherings, one for each part of the process. An exercise I call the "history grid" is the central activity for your gathering of your wider circle of leaders. But first, you will need to lay some groundwork with this group.

First part (about an hour and a quarter)

The first part of this larger learning event follows roughly the same format as your first board conversation, even though board members will be present. Going through a similar process will reinforce their learning. In addition, their leadership role will be enhanced if they participate knowledgeably in this wider event, and they will benefit from hearing what other leaders say in response to questions they have already considered.

Introduction (about 10 minutes)
• Prayer, biblical reflection, or meditation.
• Introduce the learning team.
• Review the Learning Goals for the whole process and the Five Steps (titles only) found at the beginning of this chapter. Let people know that this session will focus on the first and second goals.

- Brief silent reflection and "one minute sharing" with one other person as indicated in the suggested board format (page 74).

Presentation of the four size categories (about 15 minutes)
- Either an oral presentation or video segment "1a." (See board format, pages 74-76.)

Discussion (about 10 minutes)
- Ask participants to think for a moment about the size designation (among the four you have introduced) that best describes the congregation they identified in the reflection exercise
- Ask participants to raise their hands if the first significant congregation they experienced was family size. In the same way, have people raise their hands in turn for pastoral, program, and corporate size. Record the totals on a chart pad, using the top line of a grid as shown in figure 9.

Figure 9
Size Identification Chart

	Family	Pastoral	Program	Corporate
My past church				
Our church now				

- Now pose the question: "Which size does our congregation most resemble today?" Go through a show of hands for each category, just as you did in the previous step. Record the totals for each category. You will have time for a few comments from participants about why they voted the way the did. Let them know that you are just asking for a few initial thoughts and that after a couple of minutes you'll be adding another layer to the conversation. (There is not time for a long debate or an attempt to reach consensus.)

Presentation of plateau zone concept (about 10 minutes)
• From chapter 1, read aloud the first paragraph of the section entitled "The Pastoral-to-Program Plateau Zone" (pages 10 and 11). (Or you can show segment "1b" of the video at this point).

Discussion (about 20 minutes)
• At the top of a chart pad, write the heading, "Signs that we might be experiencing a size plateau."
• Ask the group to identify any signs of a size plateau that seem to apply to your own congregation.
• Write down exact words and phrases group members contribute
• Show the group the 30-year attendance chart you have prepared. Allow a brief discussion.
• Take a break.

Second part (about 90 minutes)

In this section, you will be asking leaders to reflect on the history of the congregation, using mainly the information they carry around in their minds and hearts. Instead of deferring to an "official" historian (if you have one) to provide all the information, you want participants in this session to become aware of their own impressions—no matter how incomplete or inaccurate these may be from a factual point of view.

To prepare for this session, you may want to interview your congregation's historian in advance to get some baseline information and his or her impressions of what this history might mean for the present. This would serve two purposes: to discover a basic time line of major events that could be helpful to the group, and to "release" the historian from needing to dominate the conversation. Ask your historian to allow the group to share their own impressions first, without "corrections." Toward the end of the event, you can invite him or her to comment briefly, offering some missing pieces or another interpretation of the story. Other occasions can always be planned to continue this conversation in more depth if there seems to be sufficient energy for it in the group.

Some congregations have an officially designated historian or archivist. In other churches, the historian or archivist is an informal role in the system, filled by the person who knows the most stories. This person may be a present member, a former member who now lives in a retirement facility, or a long-tenured member of the staff who has collected the lore. Occasionally, a congregation has no effective custodian of its history, perhaps because some traumatic event has demolished the cohort of long-term members. Through denominational archives, town historical societies, neighboring pastors, retired clergy, and elders in retirement facilities, a learning team could begin to reestablish that link. Of course, a careful search of the files, the closets, and the attic will often yield clues to past eras in the congregation's life.

Figure 10 provides the basic format for the history discussion. Some churches have more than one set of "glory days." It is essential to look at the most recent glory days (often, but not always, the 1950s). But you may decide in advance that there is another era you should look at as well. If that's the case, add another column to the chart, and work in four subgroups when you do the process outlined below. Make sure you have a copy of this chart for each person, and a very large version of it on the wall (perhaps the size of four pieces of chart paper in a square.) You will want to hold this session in a large room where there will be plenty of space for the group to spread out.

Figure 10
History Analysis Chart

	Founding Era	Glory Days	Present
What was going on in our context? • Local community • Wider culture • Wider church			
How did we view our distinctive "calling" as a congregation? Clues: • Name • Location • Building style & size • Clergy • Primary programs			
What was our definition of "right size"? How was our size affected by trends in our context? How did our size serve or hinder our calling?			

- Set the tone for the exercise: "We are going to be looking at the way this congregation has thought about itself over time. As we talk about the way the congregation defined itself in different historical eras, it's our impressions that matter, not what is written down in some book or document. So please share your impressions—no matter how new you may be to the church or how little you feel you know about its past."

- Hand out the blank grid to everyone and briefly explain each box on the left. (Some sample responses are offered in figure 11 to help you understand what fits in each box.)

- Define the eras you are going to look at. The person leading the meeting might say: "By 'founding era,' we mean the 1890s." I find that it works best if the learning team defines in advance when the most recent—other than now—"glory days" occurred (a decision you can check out with the larger group before you go into groups to work). Your 30-year attendance chart might provide a clue; so might the portrait of a beloved pastor on the wall. Basically, you are looking for the era that the largest proportion of the congregation might remember as the "good old days," about which there may still be some mourning or nostalgia.

- Identify the longest-attending person in the room. Then identify the newest church participant in the room. Ask them to stand on opposite sides of a large open area.

- Ask everyone else to line up in between these two people, based on when they started attending. (Chaos will ensue for a few minutes.)

- When people are more or less in a line, ask them to count off—1, 2, 3, 1, 2, 3.... (If you wish to reflect on two sets of "glory days," count to four.) Then ask people to move themselves into groups based on their numbers (still standing). This will result in three or four groupings with a wide mix of tenures in each.

- Assign each group one column on the grid (founding era, glory days, or now). Explain that they will spend the next 15 minutes filling in the three boxes in the column they have been assigned. Appoint one reporter for each group (a member of the learning team or someone else who will listen well and reflect the group conversation accurately).

- Send each group to a different part of the room to sit down and work.

Groups work (about 15 minutes, plus 5 minutes grace period to finish and return)

Reporters share findings of group (about 5 minutes each)
- Let people know there will be five minutes to hear the report of each group. Keep the reporting moving along.
- Record on chart pad key words and phrases for each box. (Another member of the team may want to take notes on a pad, so that key phrases are captured for later even if they don't get onto the chart.)
- Thank each group for their great work.

Explore (about 15 minutes)
- Engage in dialogue with the group about the meaning of what they see on the chart. Often, the group working on the present has had a difficult time focusing a call; typically, they generate a long list of activities with no real focus. You may want to indicate that part of the purpose of this eight-month process is to discover what that focus might be.
- Invite your official historian to add other perspectives and information.

Closing comments (5 minutes)
- Review on a chart pad the next steps your learning team and board will be taking as you complete this course. Let these leaders know how you will keep them informed as the work goes forward.

Follow-up after event
- Create a mailing list of all those who attended this event.
- Write up some of your findings and observations from this event (see guidelines in next section), including a transcript of the grid responses. Send these out by first-class mail with return postcards for comment. It is worth this small investment in postage to communicate your seriousness about keeping leaders informed and getting maximum response.

Figure 11
Sample Grid from an Episcopal Church in a New England Town

	Founding Era (Around 1900)	Glory Days (Early 1950s)	Present
Context	• Small New England town (founded 1650) steeped in history • Close to a major city • Surrounded by farm country • Congregational and UU the main churches • Town attracted "Newfies" & "Novies" (Canadian immigrants) moving out from the city	• Great wave of post-war migration from cities turns town into an inner-ring suburb • Many new families with children • Challenge to sense of community was met by new alliances; e.g., Protestants and Catholics join to place a creche on the town green at Christmas	• New wave of growth: affluent, managerial folk drawn by schools, location, feeling of community • Ways town used to build community don't work any more • Big fight over creche on town green reflects diversity in wider culture as well as in town
Congregation	• Episcopal church a "newcomer" in old town • Located up a side street (not a dominant presence) • Naturally attracted the Canadians (Anglican)	• Rapid growth • Long-tenured pastor worked with developers (who were members) to build a bigger church across the street • New building more austere: "like a Yankee meetinghouse"	• Wrestling for several years with diverse needs in worship • Recently established a second major Sunday service • Stressful; some older members feel intense grief or anger over changes

(Figure 11 continues on following page)

(Figure 11 continued)

	Founding Era	Glory Days	Present
Congregation *(continued)*	• Brought together farmers, blue-collar workers with other residents • Paternal, protecting style of clergy • Emphasis on community; everybody knew they belonged	• Newcomers and old-timers still found sense of belonging, but previous coherence was somewhat strained • Educating children a central concern; new education wing planned	• Our call today may still have to do with belonging, building community, but how do we do it in these new circumstances?
Right Size	• Small, intimate building (wood, gothic); just right for 100 people • Pastoral-sized congregation • One pastor who knew everyone • Church seems to have provided a small "alternative space" (physical, religious, ethnic), protecting people who were different in some way from the norm	• Grew to program size with the baby boom, then dropped off from mid-1960s onward (trend similar to other mainline churches) • By the time new wing was finished, it was too much to support—was rented during week • Never really settled fully into program size self-image and style	• We're unsettled about size • New worship service has grown, now exceeds the other • We worry that the new people will leave when they perceive the underlying stress • Our pastor wants us to grapple with these growth decisions together; some think he should be more directive

Task 2c: Update and summarize team learnings about congregation and context.

Create a brief discussion paper that captures the points that seem most important and interesting from your exploration so far. Remember that this document doesn't have to include answers if they are not yet emerging naturally from the conversation. For the congregation described in the sample grid, the learning team might begin their discussion paper this way: "An Episcopal presence came fairly late to our historic Yankee town. Our church was a newcomer on the scene, and gave public expression to a minority faith tradition. Other people who didn't fit the town mold—for example, Canadian immigrants, blue-collar workers, farmers, seemed to find a place of belonging here. Throughout our history, we continued to create a place of belonging for the town's newcomers—especially when the large wave of population came into the town in the 1950s. Our challenge now is to create a 'place of belonging' in a brand new set of circumstances." Below, I have included an excerpt of a short paper that another congregation's learning team developed after leaders reflected on results of the history grid exercise. The team used this paper to spark further conversation throughout the congregation about the question of calling. Suggestions about those conversations are found in task 2e.

OUR DISTINCTIVE CALLING AT MAPLE STREET CHURCH

Maple Street Congregational Church in Danvers [Massachusetts] has a *Goodly Heritage*. We were founded because 42 parishioners broke away from the then only Congregational church in Danvers in 1844. The reason for the break was their stand on abolition. These 42 men and women believed strongly enough that slavery should be abolished that they were willing to take a stand and form a new church. The willingness to stand up for our beliefs carries over to this day. We are a congregation that believes in justice and peace. We have never been afraid to confront issues outside of the church such as during the Vietnam War when our then minister used the pulpit to raise our awareness of the issues.

We are a *Constant Congregation*. Many of our parishioners have been members all their lives as were their families before them. Our church building was destroyed by fire twice and twice the people of the parish rallied together to rebuild. The attitude of the congregation over the years could be described as enthusiastic, creative, innovative, caring and involved. We have always reached out into the local area and wider community. Our mission outreach is outstanding. In the recent past we were able to facilitate the relocation of two Cambodian families into our community. More recently we have been helping families who are on welfare and enrolled in educational programs to become self-sufficient by aiding them in finding housing, providing furniture and financial support as well as spiritual support.

During the founding era of Maple Street Church, people could walk to church on Sunday. Its location in the center of town made it a logical place for the center of activities. Over the years the town grew and parishioners found themselves some distance from the church, but the automobile made it possible for people who lived further away to come to church. During the 1960s and 1970s, Danvers grew rapidly. Much of the old farmland was turned into housing developments. That rapid increase was beneficial to our church in the form of increased membership. There were two services each Sunday and many group activities throughout the week.

Today growth has slowed considerably (not much land left to build on) and the population is about 27,000 people. There are eight churches in town of various denominations, one of which is the original Congregational church. That is also a UCC church. As in many communities, church is no longer the primary focus for many people. Young families are busy with their children's sports and other activities, some of which take place on Sunday mornings. Sunday morning worship no longer has the priority it once did. In most households, both parents work and that leaves little time for church programs during the week. The world of audio and visual technology has carried us far beyond the border of Danvers, and there are many areas vying for our attention.

Our Sunday school and youth groups have grown considerably over the past several years due to the hiring of a very talented and enthusiastic CE director. We also have a dynamic group of leaders for this group. This is bringing young families into the church. The idea of adding a worship service on Sunday afternoons just before the youth group meets is already in the planning stages. Although we must not let up in this important growth area, another opportunity has opened up for us. A retirement/assisted living complex is being built in an adjacent community, which will eventually consist of 12 buildings. Currently two buildings are finished and a third will be completed soon. This is a community for people 65 and over, many of who are coming from distant cities and towns. We have always been a church that has reached out into the community, and here is our chance to continue.

Task 2d: Assess and summarize barriers to growth.

This book contains two different resources for examining barriers to growth. Chapter 2 describes six of these barriers, and suggests some ways of addressing them. The System Change Index (appendix E) provides a framework for describing where your congregation is located in its process of organizational transition.

Prepare.
- Team members should study chapters 2 and 3, and individually work through the System Change Index.
- Gather as a team to list the kinds of data you can easily get—such as seating capacity—that will aid in your assessment, and assign team members to gather it. As you go along, you will probably continue to generate questions and collect data. Keep your data-gathering as simple as possible. Sometimes the congregation's anxiety causes the team to feel they must "prove scientifically" that the church should change size. Relax—it can't be done! This change is a matter of vocation, not statistical proof.

Identify barriers.
- This discussion of barriers may continue over several meetings, as needed.
- List the six barriers from chapter 2 on your chart pad, including the subheadings. (For example, for barrier 3, you would put up the major heading—"Space effectively filled up"—and list underneath the specific areas to assess (worship, parking, education, fellowship, office).
- Identify the strongest barriers that are operating today to prevent your

congregation from growing numerically. Do this by giving each team member five "votes" to distribute over the entire list (including specific subheadings; you can vote, for example, for "parking" as a specific item). Each member should spread the five votes over five different items—this will help facilitate consensus better than a process where someone can apply five votes to one item.

- Discuss the results. Especially for the most frequently selected items, ask why members thought each item was so important.
- On a sheet of paper, list all the barriers that got at least one vote— starting with the one that received the most. As you list them, add a descriptive word or sentence from your conversation. For example, instead of just listing "parking," you might say: "People who arrive after 9:45 A.M. must walk across a dangerous road to get to church."
- Next (perhaps at a subsequent meeting), share and discuss your ratings on the System Change Index. Look for consensus on each of the nine factors, and note the elements of each factor that seem most relevant to your own congregation.
- Look first at any factor your team has rated "low." Is there something you have identified that is not already included on your list from the previous exercise? If so, add it along with an appropriate description. (You may also find that you want to modify the language of the existing statements to reflect what you learned from the SCI exercise.)
- Look now at any factor your team has rated "medium"—particularly, the elements that lowered the rating. Something may emerge from this examination that you want to add to your list of key items.

In the box below, you will see one learning team's initial list of barriers to growth—items gleaned from chapter 2 and from the System Change Index.

ONE LEARNING TEAM'S LIST OF BARRIERS TO GROWTH

- We are willing to grow, but we need a more specific plan. Our church would be in category "B1" of Alan Klaas's framework. (See page 18.)
- Once children leave near the beginning of the service, the front of church looks quite empty.
- Newcomers don't know how to find parking in back; latecomers may have to park further down the street and walk back.
- Sunday school space is beginning to feel cramped; dividers do not muffle sound.
- No office space for additional staff; storage is also a problem.
- After first day's welcome, newcomers left on their own—no programs to see to it that they become involved.
- We have little knowledge of members' gifts and talents. Our time-talent surveys haven't worked. Same leaders do many things, becoming burned out.
- Adult study programs are poorly attended.
- We expect our pastor to be there for us at all times. Don't know how pastor and congregation might accept a changing role.
- Few small groups for adults.
- Most committees don't live up to their potential.
- When people join a committee, they often have little idea what it does or how it functions. The committee chair may not have the training to guide others.
- Board would benefit from more training.

Assign priority to the barriers. Having made a full list, go through and identify barriers of special importance.

- Some barriers have greater strategic priority; that is, their removal might release the congregation's potential for solving other growth-related problems. Ask each team member individually to choose the three items from the list that seem most strategic. As team members read off their three choices, place *S* marks next to the

appropriate statements. A particular statement may be chosen by more than one member—if so, put additional *S* marks next to that item.
- Your congregation is more ready to address some of these barriers than others. Readiness comes from several sources:
  — Member awareness that a problem exists
  — Lay leader motivation to address the problem
  — Clergy motivation to address the problem
  — The availability of necessary information, ideas, and resources
  Reviewing the whole list once again, ask team members to choose the three items your congregation seems most ready to address. Place an *R* next to the appropriate item on your list each time a team member names it as one of their three.

Summarize. Using this list, draft a short paper that identifies and describes in detail three to five key barriers your congregation would need to address in the next two years in order to remove the "glass ceiling." Or, to put it another way, what would it take to attract and retain the next 50 people God wants to send you?

- Start with any barriers that have received both *S* and *R* markings from the team—that is, items of high strategic importance that the congregation may also be ready to tackle. If you have not marked any items with both letters, make sure your short list includes at least one "readiness" item and one "strategic" item.
- Mail this discussion paper out to the list of people in your wider circle of leaders. Again, include a response card, and send it first class.

Task 2e: Foster conversation about findings to date.

The two discussion papers you have created (one based on the "history grid," the other identifying barriers to growth) can now be used to stimulate conversation throughout the congregation. Here are a few ideas about how that might happen. Choose the ones that seem most appropriate to the style and needs of your own church. One tip—make it clear to any group you meet with that it is *not* their job to edit the document. Let them know that you will simply be soliciting responses and answering questions in preparation for a later document that will come back to everyone (i.e., the draft plan in step 4).

"Cottage meetings." Some congregations like to organize small-group listening sessions in members' homes, making sure each member is invited to a particular gathering. It is best if two members of the learning team can be present for each of these chats to explain what has been happening, solicit response, and write down comments to take back to the team. This conversation will go most smoothly if every group contains several people from your wider leadership circle who took part in the "history grid" conversation. Take a relaxed and inquisitive stance: "We want to let you know what we've been learning so far, and we want to hear what additional thoughts you may have."

Visits to existing groups. Sometimes the "cottage meeting" structure feels too elaborate and labor intensive; instead, you can make a list of all the groups—formal and informal—that gather in your congregation. Ask the leader of each group if you might come as guests to chat with the members about what the learning team has been finding. Again, it is best if two members of a learning team can make this visit—it's good to have support, and four ears are better than two.

Classes or forums. Adult education groups are often happy to make a contribution to this kind of congregational learning. You can involve existing groups in "studying" and responding to your documents; or you could schedule a few special forums for discussion. Ask your church school and youth leaders to help you involve youngsters in conversation about the congregation's story—perhaps they could study and illustrate key moments that express the congregation's central calling. (Maple Street Church's founding by abolitionist Christians, and its work of resettling refugees, would both lend themselves to a dramatic presentation.)

Worship service. Some congregations would enjoy hearing the team's findings in a brief, well-prepared presentation during worship (possibly in place of the sermon one Sunday). Lay voices are the most effective. This could be placed in the context of a scriptural reflection or a time of prayer. You might provide people with index cards and pencils so they can note comments and questions to share with the team afterward.

Newsletter or special congregational mailing. As a supplement to these face-to-face settings for conversation, you will want to circulate a summary of you findings in print. Pick a few of the most interesting and suggestive stories from the history grid exercise to pass along in writing—the average member is much more interested in a story than in a treatise.

Visual display in a public area. Create an attractive display of the congregation's "time line," with a collection of photos and memorabilia to make it visually interesting. Make a poster or banner that expresses the sense of calling you are discovering. Design a humorous display of "hurdles" to growth, or build a church model with an actual "glass ceiling" as part of a presentation on the barriers you are discovering. Most people remember what they see much better than what they read.

STEP 3:
EXPLORE THE UNIQUE CHARACTER
OF OUR COMMUNITY CONTEXT.

In the history grid exercise, you have already begun to describe your local community and wider context. Now it is time to check and refine your perceptions of what is going on around you.

Task 3a: Identify trends in the wider culture

Some of these trends have probably already come up in your discussions, but now would be a good moment to step back and see how others may be having an impact on your congregation.

- Appendix G contains a "trend scan" article from the Alban Institute journal, *Congregations.* Your team may wish to discuss this article to look for relevant material.
- If you prefer a visual presentation, the video *Living into the New World: How Cultural Trends Affect Your Congregation*[9] would provide your learning team (and perhaps other groups within the congregation) with a fascinating evening of reflection.

- For an in-depth written presentation, *In Search of the Unchurched: Why People Don't Join Your Congregation*[10] lists and discusses 22 cultural transitions congregations are coping with today.

Whatever resource you use, make sure you finish by identifying the top three to five cultural trends that are affecting your congregation's life and ministry today.

Task 3b: Check your perceptions of your community context using a demographic profile.

When you are ready to look at statistical information about your community, you may want to order a demographic profile from one of the companies that prepares them especially for religious congregations. A "Ministry Area Profile" from the organization called Percept[11] will cost your church several hundred dollars (unless your denomination has an arrangement for obtaining this resource at a reduced cost). I have found their material far more focused and helpful than other statistical reports I have seen, but be warned: you will receive far more information than most people can possibly assimilate. I usually ask congregations to focus their attention on the "Snapshot" page, which summarizes critical information quite succinctly. Appendix H shows a sample of such a page. Your learning team can work back from the "Snapshot" into the extensive supporting material to answer questions of particular relevance.

One of the most important kinds of information you will get from a Percept "Ministry Area Profile" is a list of key lifestyle segments in your community. This is located in the upper right-hand corner of the "Snapshot" shown in appendix H. An extensive marketing database divides the U.S. population into 50 subcultures. "Lifestyle segment" is the technical name for one of these groups. As an example, look at a few of the lifestyle segments that one congregation (which I have dubbed "Holy Trinity, Jackson Harbor") discovered within a 10-mile radius of their church. This description is their own summary of what they learned by studying their Percept profile.

OUR COMMUNITY'S KEY LIFESTYLE SEGMENTS
Holy Trinity, Jackson Harbor

"Urban Senior Life" adults are located at the northern edge of Jackson Harbor. Nationally, this group includes many people of our denomination. Adult theological discussion groups are among their expectations of a church. Current programming at Holy Trinity seems to match the needs of this segment most closely.

"Established Empty Nesters" are located in the area along the lake. This demographic segment comprises one-third of the population within 10 miles of the church. We should pay closer attention to the younger end of this group (in their 40s and early 50s). Among other things, this group tends to look for spiritual retreats as part of a church program.

"New Beginning Urbanites" are located from Jackson Harbor into the eastern edge of Brownsville. Nationally, more than half of this group rents, and many are divorced. This group tends to look for spiritual growth opportunities, along with help adjusting to divorce. The new multi-congregation youth ministry that Holy Trinity supports may be ministering with some families in this segment.

"Established Country Families" are located in the direction of Hartfield. This segment is quite mixed economically and educationally. They are concerned about children, parenting, and schools, and tend to be looking for spiritual teaching. The new youth ministry may also touch the concerns of these families.

Holy Trinity had selected a 10-mile radius as their study area. I would generally suggest that you create what Percept calls a "custom polygon"—an area bounded by a tailor-made combination of roads, rivers, town lines, or other features of your community—rather than using zip codes or automatically assuming that your ministry area fits exactly into your municipal boundaries. A custom polygon presses you to examine your assumptions more closely about the real area in which you minister. Your pin-map will help you design this polygon.

Task 3c: Check your perceptions of the context using community leader interviews.

This method produces more than information—it builds relationships.

- Make a list of four to seven community leaders from different sectors of life. Possible candidates might be: school superintendent, police chief, head of social services, town planner, a denominational official familiar with your area, and a few neighboring religious leaders.
- Assign one or two team members to handle each interview.
- Schedule a 30-minute appointment with each community leader.
- Tell the leader right at the beginning that you have two basic questions to cover during this short interview:
    — What impressions—if any—do you have of our congregation?
    — What unmet needs do you see in our community?
- I strongly suggest that you do not ask: "What should our church be doing?" I have known many community leaders to balk at a request to tell the church what its business should be. That's your job. Ask them to talk about what they know best: the conditions and needs they confront every day in their own work.
- Be prepared for some awkward moments when you ask for impressions of your congregation—these leaders may not know who you are, where you are located, or what you have ever done as a church. Asking this question gives you a reality check on whether your congregation has much of a "profile" in the wider community—and whether the information others have about you is correct. Thank them for whatever they offer.
- From the notes you have taken during the interview, write up a brief summary of the responses you received to your two questions, using as many of the person's own words and phrases as you can.
- Bring these reports back to the learning team for discussion.

Task 3d: Foster conversation about findings to date.

From the options discussed in task 2e, select appropriate ways to involve other leaders with your findings. Use as many different means of communication as possible—it's hard to tell what will get through to different sorts of people.

Step 4:
Articulate Your Congregation's
Particular Vocation (Calling)
within Your Context Today.

This is not a brand new step in the process—you've been working on aspects of this challenge all along. By now, you should have received some helpful feedback from board members, your wider circle of leaders, and members-at-large about your first discussion paper (the one based on your history grid exercise) and on your list of key barriers to numerical growth beyond the current plateau zone. This is the time to crystallize your learning in a more polished statement of vocation and an overall plan to "step into" that vocation more fully. The work of step 4 would best be done in a 24-hour retreat, because the components of prayer and creativity are so important.

Task 4a: Develop (further) your statement of your congregation's calling today.

Individual discernment. Before you meet as a team, or as part of your 24-hour retreat, set aside some time for individual discernment about your congregation's call. Here is an exercise you can use:

INDIVIDUAL EXERCISE IN DISCERNMENT

Set aside half an hour, at the time of day when you are most likely to experience creative quiet. Put yourself in an environment that supports relaxed reflection. Have in front of you several pieces of unlined paper and some writing/drawing instruments, as well as the results of the history grid exercise.

Five minutes: Breathe deeply, and ask for the breath of God to fill your body, mind, and heart—releasing anxiety about the "product" of your reflection. Trust that whatever comes will be fruitful in some way.

Five minutes: Ask for a Spirit of discernment to grasp the pattern in God's creative work—your congregation's whole life span. Draw (in any way you wish) that life span on one piece of paper.

Fifteen minutes: As you look at the life span of your congregation, fill in as many of the following short-answer questions as you can without effort.

If this congregation's life span were a novel, what would the title be?

_____

What theme song or hymn might accompany this life span?

_____

What visual symbol or image would sum up the life of this congregation? (Draw it in some way on a piece of paper.)

What biblical story, character, or situation does your congregation's life span remind you of? _____

Five minutes: Give thanks for whatever has happened—even if you have drawn a total blank, or even if you "blew" the quiet by answering the phone. Trust God to use whatever has happened to stir your mind and heart toward a discernment of the deep spiritual meaning hidden in your congregation's life span.

Look for powerful words and images. When you gather as a learning team, share what came to you in your individual time of reflection. Then make a list of the most powerful words and images that emerged. After a short break, go back to your transcription of the "history grid" conversation and the discussion paper you created from it. Once again, look for the most powerful words and images. As a model, notice again how Maple Street Church (pages 89 and 90) told specific stories from the past, named specific ministries though the years that epitomized the church's sense of vocation, and generated some memorable language ("goodly heritage," "constant congregation") to characterize the congregation's self-understanding. I encouraged this team to come up with one more colorful phrase that might express the spirit of outreach (both invitation and service) that their paper discusses at some length.

Build your emerging statement around that powerful material. Maple Street Church could have organized its points in several different ways. But people don't remember a list of points—they remember powerful words and images. Even now (some months after the course ended in which Maple Street participated), I have little trouble remembering their two key phrases and their excitement about reaching emerging populations around them. Avoid generic language; instead, choose phrases and images that are somehow particular to your congregation's style and experience. Just as the tiny church I mentioned earlier took Van Morrison as a sort of patron saint ("We're cranky and cantankerous, but still there's this longing for God"), you can find a saint, a theme song, a bible passage, or a symbol that resonates with your congregation's special personality.

Task 4b: Develop a draft plan for further learning and action.

Here is a general format for your plan. During your 24-hour retreat, or at a meeting of the learning team, begin to pull together all the elements using the following outline.

OUTLINE FOR DRAFT PLAN

A. Our historic identity and vocation
What is the distinctive calling that we have discovered in our congregation's story? What symbols and phrases express that calling powerfully for us?
(You have worked on this element in the previous step of the process. Here you will only need to summarize it.)

B. Our present demographic and cultural context
What is different about our local community and our wider culture today? What populations do we have a special vocation to reach now?
(Your scan of cultural trends, pin-map, demographic profile, and community interviews should help you to answer this question.)

C. Obstacles to growth/passive barriers
What would we have to change in order to reach and retain the next 50 people God wants to send us?
(Refer to your discussion paper on passive barriers, and to the responses you have received.)

D. Assessment of readiness
How prepared are we (clergy, lay leadership, congregation) to make those changes? How well do we handle difference and disagreement? Do we have the self-confidence to tackle a big project?
(See the next section for suggestions.)

E. Next steps
What should we do in the next three months? What can we accomplish within the next year? What long-term goals need preparatory study and discussion, and how will we structure that learning?
(See the next section for suggestions.)

Assessing readiness. To complete this part of the plan, reflect with the team on your whole learning experience over the past months, and also your experience of other change projects your congregation has tackled. Think about:

- The responses members have made to your discussion papers.
- The climate and tone of the learning experiences you have offered to the board and to the wider circle of leaders.
- Reactions of members to the sharing you have done at worship, in the newsletter, and so forth.
- Your own feelings of confidence or apprehension about proceeding to work on size transition tasks.

It may seem a little strange to describe the readiness level in your plan, but this may be a very helpful contribution to the congregation's life. Here is a sample statement that a learning team might make in response to the readiness question:

> The question of numerical growth has been a taboo subject for years, because pastoral size just seemed "right" to many of us. Now more and more leaders agree that we can't call ourselves "welcoming to newcomers" if we turn a blind eye to the seating and parking problems. Either option for increasing physical capacity—extending the building or adding a worship service—will generate some distress, and our wider leadership circle isn't quite confident yet that we can respond well to the increased anxiety. This project will only succeed if we practice some new ways of working together. That is why the proposed next steps include a workshop for leaders and members on handling differences, and development of a covenant stating our values and practices for times of disagreement. No matter what we decide to do about growth, this work will strengthen us as a faith community. It will also provide relationship tools our members can use in family, work and civic settings.

If your issues resemble the ones in the sample statement, you may want to consider using one of three fine resources. *Behavioral Covenants in Congregations*[12] provides conceptual background and a practical framework for negotiating new "ground rules" for healthy disagreement. *Congregational*

Fitness: Healthy Practices for Layfolk[13] empowers the individual leader or member to try new behaviors that will contribute to the health of the whole church body. *Difficult Conversations*[14] describes how congregations got into—and can get out of—avoiding controversial subjects; the author shows how to create a respectful environment where different viewpoints can be heard and honored.

Identifying next steps. Your plan may include steps of three different kinds.

- Steps for further learning. On some important issues, your team may conclude that an intentional learning process should continue, perhaps using resources and suggestions you did not have time for in this cycle. If, for example, your board is wondering about starting an additional worship service, but isn't sure what style it should be, a new cycle of learning about this subject might be very helpful. (Appendix I contains a chapter from *The In-Between Church* that deals with this subject—a very common issue for churches to face in the pastoral-to-program plateau.)
- Steps for further discernment. Sometimes a learning process like the one you are leading causes the congregation to realize that it faces a big decision. (A very dramatic example would be whether the congregation should sell its current property and move to a new location to accommodate growth.) In that case, you may be sketching out steps in a formal discernment process focused on that one question.
- Steps for action. If you have identified some barriers of strategic importance that the congregation is ready to tackle, action steps will be appropriate.

Each type of step may be proposed in any time frame of your plan—three months, one year, or longer term.

For each step you propose, indicate who will be responsible to implement it. Sometimes that will be an existing group. In other cases, new ad hoc teams may be needed to pursue a specific project. Make it clear that the learning team per se will go out of existence once the plan is adopted. This helps other leaders to realize that their ownership and follow-through are needed to implement the plan.

Task 4c: Foster conversation about findings to date.

- Again see the suggestions in step 2e.
- At this point, you will conduct another full hour of conversation with the board.
- Make sure they have received your most recent statement of vocation and your draft plan well in advance of this meeting.
- Begin the discussion with a time of biblical reflection and prayer for discernment.
- Remind the board that the purpose is not to edit a document, but to discuss the substance of your proposals in preparation for formal action later.
- After the board conversation, reflect together as a team on any final revisions you wish to make before the work is presented for action.

STEP 5:
BRING THE REVISED STATEMENT
OF VOCATION AND DRAFT PLAN
TO THE BOARD FOR FORMAL ACTION.

This step marks the end of the cycle of learning envisioned in this book. But for your congregation, it is the beginning of a new phase of learning, discernment, and action—a commencement of sorts.

Board action. In some congregations, the board vote will be a foregone conclusion by now. In other situations, you will still find yourselves negotiating anxieties right down to the wire.

- If you sense that you are in the latter situation, you may want to speak with each board member individually before the meeting, to make sure you know what thoughts and concerns they will be bringing to the meeting.
- Your goal is not to make everyone happy—that project is doomed before it begins. Rather, as you prepare for this meeting, focus on the work of honoring different viewpoints and addressing substantive concerns.

What if? If your proposals are not adopted at the meeting where you expected positive action, treat this result as more data about the state of the system, and keep working.

- At that point, you may want to request that your board's executive committee or another subgroup join with the team in a "conference committee" to fashion a version of your material that will be able to gain board endorsement.
- Remember, you have not failed if your board says to you: "We're not ready yet for what you have proposed." You can always drop back a step, and propose whatever kind of work will help build readiness for future decisions.
- The real success is that you are engaging them with questions about your congregation's future—these seeds may sprout later in ways you would never have expected.

From board to congregation. In many congregations, the board's action will be a prelude to a wider congregational meeting in which the assembled members are asked to endorse the project.

- To a large extent, the congregational meeting should be made up of your "wider circle of leaders"; your learning team may want to speak personally to key people in the wider circle to encourage their attendance.
- In advance of the meeting, make up a list of the most likely questions, comments, and concerns.
- Think about which person from the wider circle of leaders would be the most effective voice to respond to a particular concern. You can ask individual leaders to be ready to speak to certain issues if they come up: "Jane, if someone voices a fear about dividing the congregation with two worship services, would you be willing to share how your own thinking has changed on this matter?"
- You may want to think about some hymns that might be appropriate to sing after the congregation takes action, to mark the significance of these decisions. If the conversation has been difficult, you will want to sing something that honors that difficulty—for example, "Blest be the tie that binds" or "Ubi caritas" might be more appropriate than "Onward, Christian soldiers."

Celebration and implementation. Endorsement is a beginning and an ending.

- You team's final task is to mark the transition to the implementation stage by saying good-bye. Before the congregational meeting ends, thank the members and staff for their help in the process.
- Hold one more meeting of the learning team that is focused on the theme of letting go. While individual members may decide to participate in aspects of implementation, the learning team as a group must entrust the work to others and to God. Plan an appropriate ritual to mark this moment of ending—including a chance for each person to say what it has meant to them to take part in the process.
- Here is a prayer, attributed to King Alfred the Great, that I sometimes ask groups to pray with me at the beginning and end of this kind of work.

To see thee is the end and the beginning.
Thou carriest me and thou goest before.
Thou art the journey and the journey's end. Amen.

The Foundations Course: Cornerstone of an Adult Faith Formation Strategy

A s a congregation attempts to set a new spiritual climate and to em-power laity with practical knowledge of the Christian faith, the establishment of a Foundations Course may be both efficient and transformational.

(Please see following page.)

CHARACTERISTICS OF A FOUNDATIONS COURSE

Substantial	At least 20 hours of instruction
Varied	Includes prayer, faith sharing experiences, presentations, discussion, practice with various methods of prayer and Bible study, role-play of life situations, etc.
Provides memorable frameworks/concepts	Overview of the biblical story

Origins of various churches and roots of our tradition

Summary statements of Christian faith (creeds, confessions, catechisms, etc.)

Frameworks describing key arenas of Christian living, the daily ministry of the *laos*, and basic elements of spiritual practice |
| Repeated year after year | At least annually (even if only five people do it)

May be divided into three or four units, so that people can pick up one unit at a time if scheduling is difficult

Basic content remains stable |
| For all adults, not just inquirers | All adult members encouraged to take part

Also serves as a substantial reintroduction to Christian faith for newcomers, adults being baptized/confirmed, people preparing for marriage or for baptism of a child, etc. |
| Can become a standard for other responsibilities | May eventually be requested of all those who run for important offices or accept important appointments, including teaching ministries |
| Recognition | Keep records and celebrate completion! |

Adapted from Robert Gallagher, *Power from on High* (Philadelphia: Ascension Press, 1982). Out of print.

Resources for Releasing Gifts for Ministry

The following provides current listings from the Congregational Resource Guide. You can access the whole guide, which is continually expanding, at www.alban.org. Click on the Congregational Resource Guide box. These listings were found in the "Leadership" section (subheadings: gifts identification, lay ministry, and vocation) and in the "Administration" section (subheading: staffing; topic: volunteers).

Created and Called: Discovering Our Gifts for Abundant Living (book in binder format)
Jean M. Trumbauer, Author. Minneapolis: Augsburg Fortress, 1998.

True to its title, *Created and Called* emphasizes that we are cocreators with God in the continuing work of creation and healing, and that each person is gifted and called by the Creator to ministry. Unlike manuals with similar themes, *Created and Called* explains how our gifts are more than our most visible talents and skills: they include our interests, motivations, styles, values, hopes, and vulnerabilities. Recognizing that most mainline congregations do not assist members in discovering their gifts, this manual provides a comprehensive approach to recognizing traditional gifts (talents, skills, and knowledge), gifts of style (learning, personality, and motivational styles), and gifts of vulnerability (values, emotions, dreams, and wounds). It then guides users in integrating these gifts and applying them to needs in both the church and the larger community. With reflection guides, reflection exercises, samples, and a listing of further resources in each chapter, Trumbauer has provided an excellent resource for gifts identification facilitators to use in small groups, adult education curricula, and leadership programs.

How to Mobilize Church Volunteers (book)
Marlene Wilson, Author. Minneapolis: Augsburg Fortress, 1983.

Marlene Wilson asserts that church leaders who plan projects and programs should not focus on filling empty volunteer slots; instead they should identify church members' gifts, leadership styles, and needs. Using her management background, Wilson suggests guidelines for understanding personality types and improving a church's "climate" (or attitudes toward volunteering), planning methods, and mission goals. She then lists exercises that church leaders can use in motivating lay members to offer their talents in the church and community. The sample job descriptions, creativity checklist, personal action plan, and evaluation forms provide concrete ways for church members to develop a vibrant model of service.

LifeKeys: Discovering Who You Are, Why You're Here, and What You Do Best (book)
Jane A. G. Kise, David Stark, and Sandra Krebs Hirsh, Authors. Minneapolis: Bethany House Publishers, 1996.

A guide to discovering your God-given gifts. This is part of a larger set of LifeKeys resources developed by the same team. (Authors note: Like Trumbauer's *Created and Called*, LifeKeys offers a very broad definition of the word *gifts*. While Trumbauer presents a more close argued theology of giftedness, LifeKeys provides a congregation with a more accessible book for a new member orientation, cell group, or adult class.)

Sharing the Ministry: A Practical Guide for Transforming Volunteers into Ministers (book in binder format). Jean M. Trumbauer, Author. Minneapolis: Augsburg Fortress, 1999.

Moving beyond the "fill 'em and forget 'em" volunteer recruitment model, the author presents a new paradigm of volunteer ministry based on the assumptions that each person is uniquely gifted for ministry, that church ministry is shared, and that staff and lay leaders are to help identify, develop, use, and support the gifts of all members. The shift into a new volunteer ministry paradigm takes time; this manual encourages readers to begin with small steps and allow several years to implement a full shared ministry systems approach. After explaining the shared ministry systems model, Trumbauer devotes the succeeding chapters to exploring the model's processes: planning, discovering gifts, designing, recruiting, interviewing, matching, training, supervising, supporting, evaluating, and managing data. With reflection exercises, sample models, and suggestions for further resources in each chapter, the manual can be used in learning designs for two-session workshops, all-day workshops, or in-service sessions at board, committee, or staff meetings. Readers may also purchase a set of "personal reflection guides" that will facilitate gifts discernment.

What You Do Best in the Body of Christ (book)
Bruce Bugbee, Author. Grand Rapids, Mich.: Zondervan Publishing House, 1995.

This book is a practical handbook for every individual wanting to further explore his or her passion, spiritual gifts, personal style, and life calling. Bugbee takes a fresh approach to a familiar concept and provides exercises, biblical examples, and reflections which all contribute to making this publication an easy-to-read and excellent resource for anybody involved in developing equipping ministry and/or discerning their personal servant profile and calling in the body of Christ. *(Author's note: This resource is part of the Network series of resources, originally developed at Willow Creek Church.)*

Factors in the Stevenson "Margin-in-Life" Scale

Factor 1	Health	Contained the body (physical items as well as mental and general health items).
Factor 2	Self	Included items about responsibility, work life, like goals, ability to concentrate, self-confidence, adaptability to change, decision-making, and temper-control.
Factor 3	Family	Contained items concerned with the family as a whole, with children and spouses specifically, and with other relatives.
Factor 4	Religiosity/ Spirituality	Contained religiosity items, which deal with the dimensions of an organized religion, such as church membership, prayer, Bible reading, people met at church and through church-related activities. It includes the spirituality items: philosophy of life, honesty, conscience, and a personal value system.
Factor 5	Community	Contained items about the larger environment; keeping abreast of world and local news, items about neighbors and about civic activities.

For full information, see Joanne Sabol Stevenson, "Construction of a Scale to Measure Load, Power and Margin in Life," Nursing Research *31, 4 (July-August 1982).*

"Raising the Roof"
Interview Questions

1. **Interviewee**
   A. Name
   B. Phone number
   C. How long attending
   D. Current church position(s)
   E. Past church positions
   F. Age
   G. Added informally—professional background

2. **Size History of Congregation**
   I would like to understand the history of this church's thinking about growth and size change.
   A. Any initial comments?
   B. How long ago did this church start grappling with these issues? How?
   C. Is there a particular moment or event that really put questions of growth or size on the table? How?
   D. Have there ever been "camps" of opinion about whether to grow or how to grow? What were they?
   E. On a scale of 1 to 10 (1 being low), how controversial has this subject been in the past five years?

3. **Leadership**
   I assume that growth and size change requires leadership from many different places.
   A. Initial comments on who has been leading the church to grow or change size? How?

B. Comments on the role of senior pastor?
C. Moderator?
D. Primary governing board?
E. Committees and task forces?
F. Other individuals?

4. **Individual Role**
    I'd like to understand where you fit into this story.
    A. Initial comments?
    B. When did you first become conscious of this church's choices about growth and size? How?
    C. What have you done about those issues?

5. **Conflict**
    A. On a scale of 1 to 10 (1 being low), how much conflict or disagreement has there been about these issues?
    B. When did people fight or disagree?
    C. How was this handled?

6. **Authority**
    Growth involves change. Change means giving up some treasured ways of doing things. Some leaders ask: "What right do I have to ask others in this church to change?"
    A. Any thoughts?
    B. Have others ever questioned your position or wisdom on this issue?
    C. To what extent do you feel you have the right or responsibility to put growth or size change on the church's agenda?
    D. I'd like to understand the foundation on which you stand. Please rate each statement 1 to 10 (1 being a low agreement with the statement).
        1. As I see it, seeking to grow is good business strategy for the church.
        2. As I see it, seeking to grow is a biblical mandate.
        3. As I see it, seeking to grow is not an issue at all—we're just trying to manage the problems that are right in front of us.
        4. As I see it, people need spiritual help in their lives. We're supposed to find the people who need that help and offer it.

5. As I see it, my life was changed when somebody helped me find faith. I'm supposed to do that for others.
6. As I see it, the Conference (i.e., middle judicatory body) has growth as a goal, and we should cooperate with that work.
7. As I see it, being a called or elected leader means taking some heat around hard issues, including growth.
8. As I see it, leaders should only do what the congregation wants or seems comfortable with.
9. (For lay leaders.) As I see it, our minister believes we should grow, and I think we should cooperate with that effort.

7. Other

What else should I have asked? What other comments would you like to make?

System Change Index

This instrument is meant to foster conversation about the congregation's progress through the transition zone between pastoral and program size. On the chart below (figure 12), average Sunday* attendance is shown on the horizontal axis. (*See explanatory note in the Scoring and Plotting section). Possible scores from the inventory (called System Change Index values) are shown on the vertical axis. After you complete the inventory, you will plot your congregation's "location" on this chart.

The pastoral-to-program plateau zone is represented by two curved bands labeled "T1" (depicting an early stage of size transition) and "T2" (depicting an advanced stage of size transition).

The wedge-shaped area defined by two dark lines illustrates my hypothesis about potential for further growth. It is my impression that congregations located in this area of the chart may have the greatest potential for continued growth through the plateau zone, because they are changing their way of operating at about the right pace.

Congregations located below the wedge and to the right may be changing their way of operating too slowly to support their current attendance level and to allow for further natural growth. Congregations located above the wedge and to the left may not be drawing sufficient numbers to sustain a program style of operation; more work on invitation may be needed.

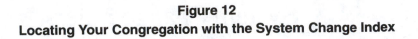

Figure 12
Locating Your Congregation with the System Change Index

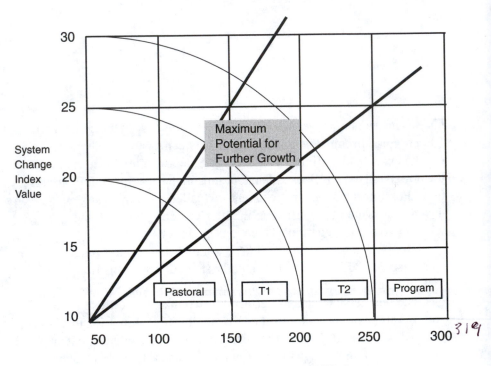

Average Attendance Last 52 Weeks

DIRECTIONS

For each factor, read all the items that might affect your congregation's score. Circle any words or phrases that describe your congregation well. Taking into account the whole list of items, rate your congregation "high," "medium," or "low" on this factor. Note your main reason(s) for your rating. (If the pastor has not used the Blanchard LBA II or SL II inventory, ignore these items.)

Factor 1: Congregational self-definition.

The story leaders tell about the congregation's size and character. Language and images used. Functioning theology about size and growth.

Our congregation rates *higher* on this factor if:
- Most of our active members accept the fact that this is no longer a small church.
- Key lay leaders often put into their own words the reasons it is right for our congregation to grow numerically at this time.
- Our boards, committees, and groups see it as their job to make room for more people in their particular areas of worship, program, and fellowship.
- When we gather informally (suppers, coffee hour, parking lot), we usually make positive comments about our numerical growth and our newer members.
- We are the sort of congregation that "steps up" to new community needs; our faith calls us to expand our capacity in response to population growth.

Our congregation rates *lower* on this factor if:
- Active members frequently say that it would be better to remain small so we can all know each other.
- Our main motivation for growth is to resolve our budget difficulties.
- Usually it is the pastor who states the reasons we should grow numerically at this time.
- A few people are thinking about growth issues, while the boards and committees mostly attend to other business.

- When we gather informally, we hear many reservations and complaints about changes related to numerical growth.

Rating: ❏ Low = 1   ❏ Medium = 2   ❏ High = 3

Reasons for rating:

Factor 2: Pastor's role.

Emphasis on pastor's role as leader, equipper, and organizer. Ability and willingness to delegate. Understanding and acceptance of this role by lay leaders and members.

Our congregation rates *higher* on this factor if:
- At least one-third of our pastor's time is spent organizing effective ministries: defining tasks, discerning gifts, recruiting leaders, establishing teams, training/coaching/mentoring new leaders, helping ongoing committees and ministries to become more effective, etc.
- Most of the pastoral care in our congregation occurs through well-organized ministries (groups, programs, and lay care teams). We expect our pastor to help us care for each other effectively.
- Our pastor experiences the work of leading and organizing as a valid and satisfying expression of ordained ministry.
- Leaders celebrate growth as an opportunity for expanding members' ministry to each other. If there were ample budget for additional clergy, the congregation would still emphasize member ministries of caring.
- Our pastor is within or above the norm in leadership style flexibility and effectiveness (as measured by the Blanchard LBA II or SL II) or is implementing a related plan to improve leadership skills.

Our congregation rates *lower* on this factor if:
- Many of our members feel neglected if the pastor has not visited with them recently.

- When confronted with administrative and political challenges occasioned by growth, our pastor is apt to say, "This isn't what I was ordained for."
- Even though we have a good lay pastoral care team, our pastor still feels guilty about not being present in every moment of need; sometimes our pastor undercuts the team by making visits that are their responsibility.
- When complaints come up about pastoral care, lay leaders hesitate to speak up and explain what is expected of the pastor in a growing congregation.
- Our pastor is currently below the norm in leadership style flexibility or effectiveness (as measured by LBA II or SL II) and we have no plan in place for skill development.

Rating: ☐ Low = 1   ☐ Medium = 2   ☐ High = 3

Reasons for rating:

Factor 3: Size of paid staff.

In the middle of pastoral size (a total attendance of 100 to 120 people), congregations are often staffed by a full-time ordained minister, a half-time secretary, a part-time custodian or cleaning service, and a musician who is compensated for a day or so each week to prepare instrumental music and rehearse the choir for one main service.

As average attendance approaches 150, a congregation that wants to support continued growth may add a half-time position on the program side (assisting pastor or lay professional), increase the level of office support, and extend a custodian's hours for building maintenance and room set-up. Having launched a children's choir or a new adult ensemble, the church may budget for an additional day of a musician's time.

As attendance approaches 200, growth cannot usually be sustained without the equivalent of at least two full-time program staff—clergy or lay; the equivalent of at least two full-time positions for office support and building maintenance; and (if there is more than one major sabbath service) the equivalent of a half-time musician.

Continued growth at an attendance of 250 will probably require the equivalent of at least: two-and-a-half program staff positions, a half-time musician, and two-and-a-half positions for office support and building maintenance.

Our congregation rates *higher* on this factor if:
• We are staffed at least to the levels suggested above for our size.
• We have undertaken serious study of staffing needs occasioned by growth and have developed a comprehensive staffing plan (including funding strategy).
• We have an able group developing personnel practices and policies.

Our congregation rates *lower* on this factor if:
• Our staffing levels fall below those suggested.
• We make our staff decisions piece-meal, without an overall assessment and plan.
• We are casual about personnel policies and practices.

Rating: ❏ Low = 1   ❏ Medium = 2   ❏ High = 3

Reasons for rating:

Factor 4: Optimum unfilled capacity at our main sabbath services/programs.

Maximum opportunity for growth occurs when 30 to 40 percent of the comfortable seating capacity is still unfilled at each Sunday* service. (*Please see explanatory note in section B on page 137.) Parking, education, and fellowship areas should also have obvious unfilled capacity every week.

These factors affect the participation level of current members as well as the congregation's permeability to newcomers.

Our congregation rates *higher* on this factor if:
- Comfortable, easily accessible seating options are visible every week at worship starting time—in each service.
- None of our services occupies less than 50 percent of seating capacity. If we have "chapel" type services (smaller gatherings at less popular hours), they take place in an appropriate-sized space. We adjust the seating arrangement in "off" seasons so that the space does not seem empty. (For example, part of our seating consists of chairs that can be removed or respaced in the summer.)
- Visitors who arrive just before the service can always find a parking space without difficulty. Current members rarely complain about parking problems.
- Our education programs for children and adults always have comfortable seating available for someone who arrives at the last minute. It is easy to get in and out of these spaces—no one feels "trapped" if they drop in to try out the program.
- Rest rooms can accommodate a crowd and are easy to find.
- Our nursery area seems calm, clean, and spacious when parents bring their children in.

Our congregation rates *lower* on this factor if:
- Any of our services is filled beyond 80 percent of its comfortable capacity (measured at 30 to 36 inches per person) on more than six Sundays* each year other than church holidays; or if any of our services is filled to less than 50 percent of comfortable capacity on more than six Sundays* other than holidays.
- Our way of involving children in worship creates double discomfort: overcrowding in the part of the service where children are present (especially if this is the opening when visitors may be seeking a seat), and a vacant feeling the rest of the time.
- Parking just before service time requires considerable effort or a long walk on more than six Sundays* other than holidays.
- People who come to adult education or social time see a cramped space with poor access to seats, refreshments, and exits (especially if they should wish to leave before the program is over).

- Rest rooms are crowded, unattractive, or hard to find.
- Parents see crowding, disorganization, or dingy facilities when they bring their children to the church school or nursery areas.

Rating: ❑ Low = 2   ❑ Medium = 4   ❑ High = 6
(Please note the doubled point values for this item.)

Reasons for rating:

Factor 5: Degree of movement toward "multicell" reality.

In a growing pastoral-size church, the small network of leaders often be-comes stressed as it tries to keep everything going. They still provide the emotional "glue" that holds the church together as a single circle of fellow-ship. In a "multicell" congregation, that informal network is replaced by fully functioning boards, committees, and ministry teams that draw new leaders from all parts of the congregation. Members accept the fact that there are distinct subcommunities within the church—often assembled around multiple major Sunday* worship services.

Our congregation rates *higher* on this factor if:
- Our boards, committees and ministry teams are well organized, and all know what each is responsible for. Attendance at meetings is consis-tently good.
- People often comment on the wealth of talent and leadership we have in this church. We have clear processes to recruit, orient, and train new board and committee members. At least 50 different adults fill some sort of leadership role.
- Whenever a major worship service is filled to 80 percent of comfort-able capacity on 6 or more nonholiday weekends a year, we start plan-ning another worship option. Because we have a shared sense of mis-sion, we still experience ourselves as a unified congregation even though people worship at different times.

- Year by year we increase the number of options for child and adult education, youth, musical participation, men's and women's fellowship, small-group sharing, and spiritual growth. We add holiday worship services as needed to provide comfortable space for everyone.
- The board no longer depends on a small "core group" of longer-term members to keep things going.

Our congregation rates *lower* on this factor if:
- Adults from about 20 households anchor almost every important ministry in the congregation and provide the nucleus of the board from year to year.
- Many people feel that the congregation could not be a healthy community if there were more than one major Sunday* worship option.
- Most of our program areas (such as men's and women's fellowships, youth, adult education, community outreach, member care, music) consist of only one group. We would rather all stay together than provide options by subdividing.
- We feel that it is too much burden on our staff and choir to add more holiday services, even though we are cramped or turn people away.
- Many of our best leaders burn out. Some then withdraw from active participation.

Rating: ❑ Low = 1   ❑ Medium = 2   ❑ High = 3

Reasons for rating:

Factor 6: Delegation of planning and change management tasks to special groups with appropriate gifts.

Timely progression from planning studies to decision to implementation, including fund development. Adequate number of self-motivated lay leaders ("change champions") guiding the political and organizational processes from phase to phase and integrating the work into a coherent effort. Willingness to learn from outside sources.

Our congregation rates *higher* on this factor if:

- Our congregation has completed or updated a long-range plan within the last three years.
- All our board and committee members know what the main long-term goals are and understand their role in implementation.
- We regularly create special groups to study specific aspects of growth, such as space, staffing, capital funding, new worship services, expanding our church school. These groups make timely recommendations that are voted upon promptly and implemented effectively.
- Our planning groups frequently learn from people outside the congregation: denominational resource persons, other congregations, professional fundraisers, organizational consultants. They find and use the best published resources in their learning.
- We have at least half a dozen well-respected leaders who are "change champions"—people with sustained energy and passion for this congregation's growth. They help lead the work from phase to phase, and are often willing to move into the next needed position of leadership (for example, a retiring board chair then leads the capital campaign). These people understand change management from their experience in community organizations, business, education, unions, or previous church involvement.

Our congregation rates *lower* on this factor if:

- We have no up-to-date long-range plan.
- Our boards, committees, and ongoing groups operate like separate organizations. They do not relate their work to commonly agreed goals or seek to collaborate with other groups. We prevent conflict by assigning each group its own turf.
- We worry a great deal about growth-related challenges, but rarely authorize a special group to study an issue and make recommendations. The board feels overwhelmed by the complexity of the change we are facing.
- We tend to suspect outside experts and doubt that any other congregation could share helpful insights with us. We always prefer home-grown wisdom.
- Our committee chairs and board members do their best while they are

in office, but we rely on the pastor and staff to provide continuity in our growth efforts. Plans made in one year often fail to be implemented once new committee members come on board.

Rating: ❑ Low = 1 ❑ Medium = 2 ❑ High = 3

Reasons for rating:

Factor 7: Growing aspirations to quality.

We aspire to quality, especially in the worship experience (including sermons, music, children's participation, cohesion of elements, climate of hospitality); nursery and education for children; educational/spiritual development of adults; and major community programming (such as support group for divorced/widowed persons, weekday nursery school).

Our congregation rates *higher* on this factor if:
- Our pastor usually spends a full day of the workweek preparing a sermon.
- Worship planning involves effective teamwork among the worship leader, preacher, musicians, lay assistants and acolytes, church school leaders, and greeters/ushers. The result is a coherent and uplifting worship experience.
- We employ specially trained/licensed professionals to supervise nursery care, and we follow clear safety policies in all our programs for children and youth.
- All our program leaders, whether paid or volunteer, have the right training, skill, and attitude for their role.
- We evaluate each program annually, and develop goals for quality improvement.

Our congregation rates *lower* on this factor if:
*   The administrative and pastoral load causes our pastor to prepare sermons at the last minute or on a day off.
*   The elements of our worship seem to be planned separately and don't "add up" to a coherent and uplifting experience. Sometimes there seems to be competition between elements, or too many elements are loaded into one service.
*   At budget time, we hear significant complaints about proposals to employ qualified nursery staff. Safety policies in our programs for children and youth are weak.
*   Since we have trouble recruiting program leaders for church school, youth, and adult education, we don't feel we can expect very much. We rarely ask these volunteers to attend training or planning sessions, or to study material on their own.
*   We evaluate by waiting for complaints, and we focus our planning on fixing the problems people seem most upset about.

Rating: ❑ Low = 1   ❑ Medium = 2   ❑ High = 3

Reasons for rating:

Factor 8: Infrastructure for member care and involvement.

Many gifted teams working on the tasks of new member incorporation, pastoral care, small groups, larger fellowship occasions, and ongoing "member ministry development" (gift identification, volunteer management, support for ministry in daily life). A reliable member database, constantly updated, is accessible to all leaders as needed.

Our congregation rates *higher* on this factor if:

- From the first day someone visits our church onward, we are organized to gather accurate information about them. We integrate this information into a well-chosen database program, and deliver information reliably to those who need it.
- Pastoral care is seen as the congregation's responsibility, with certain functions delegated to our ordained ministers. We have a specific board, committee, or lay team that designs effective ways for members to care for each other (through new member gatherings, lay visitation programs, small groups, education/support groups for people with common needs, referrals, etc.)
- We have at least two occasions every year when all our congregation's subcommunities come together for a project or celebration. If one of these is a work project (such as a parish fair), we make sure that the other is a celebration time. If necessary, we rent a large space off site to accommodate everyone.
- We are constantly learning about the gifts and interests of all our members. We do not rely on a check-off sheet; we use interactive methods such as interviews and gift identification workshops. A gifted person or team works year-round to connect members with satisfying ministries inside and outside the church.
- We give careful attention to the number of small- and large-group opportunities we have for adults, and the quality of each one. We start a new group every 6 to 12 months in order to make room for new members and emerging needs.

Our congregation rates *lower* on this factor if:

- Our lists are not accurate or up-to-date. We cannot reliably provide each group (such as the stewardship committee, church school, or new member welcomers) with current data about every person they should contact.
- We see pastoral care as the job of our ordained ministers. A few lay people may help out, but we do not have a lay-led system for member care.
- We don't bring our subcommunities together effectively in a big event every year. The ways we once came together (church school picnic, dinners, or parish fair) now reach only selected parts of the congregation. We never gather primarily for fun and celebration.

- We rely on general announcements or a check-off sheet to discover our members' gifts. We have difficulty recruiting enough people to serve as leaders and volunteers in teaching, worship, member care, community service, or board/committee positions.
- We don't evaluate or set goals for our small- and large-group opportunities, and we have not added a new group in the last 18 months.

Rating: ❑ Low = 1   ❑ Medium = 2   ❑ High = 3

Reasons for rating:

Factor 9: Conflict prevention and management.

Communication among different groups and functions. Settings where "pinches" are identified early and addressed through shared problem solving. Board and clergy competence in managing conflicts that arise. High commitment to "due process." Attention to restoring energy and trust after a difficult fight.

Our congregation rates *higher* on this factor if:
- We have an effective structure—such as a coordinating council or semi-annual planning day involving leaders from all programs—for communication, planning, calendar negotiation and problem solving.
- We look into complaints, but do not change course without an overall assessment of how things are going. We make sure we understand what is working well before we try to "fix" a problem.
- Our pastor and lay leaders are well educated about conflict in churches. They expect conflicts to arise, know how to assess the seriousness of conflict, take effective steps to reduce tension and structure problem solving, and call in appropriate help when "camps" withdraw from friendly interaction with each other.
- We guarantee "due process" to staff members, volunteers, or groups

that are criticized. We engage in fair and deliberate procedures even if some members demand immediate action.

- Few conflicts in the past decade have resulted in competing "camps." Where this has occurred, we have made clear decisions, learned from the process, rebuilt trust, and regained energy for new projects and risks.

Our congregation rates *lower* on this factor if:

- We rely on the pastor, the governing board, or appointed liaisons to guarantee communication, integration, and problem solving among programs and leaders.
- We find complaints very upsetting and expect leaders to "fix" problems right away—especially if the person seems angry or hurt.
- Our pastor and lay leaders find escalating conflict very distasteful. They put off planning a response as long as possible, and do not know how to assess their options. Leaders have not established rules for "fighting fair" in our congregation.
- Staff members and volunteer leaders cannot count on "due process" if they are criticized. Members often air complaints without using established channels, or personalize their criticisms.
- We tend to divide into competing "camps." Recent conflicts are unresolved, or, if resolved, have left us fatigued, demoralized, or nervous about new projects and risks.

Rating: ❑ Low = 1   ❑ Medium = 2   ❑ High = 3

Reasons for rating:

SCORING AND PLOTTING

A. System Change Index

Factor	Circle One for Each Factor			Enter Numerical Score for Each Factor
	Low	Medium	High	
1. Congregation self-definition	1	2	3	
2. Pastor's role	1	2	3	
3. Size of paid staff	1	2	3	
4. Physical capacity *(Point values are doubled for this item.)*	2	4	6	
5. Movement toward "multicell"	1	2	3	
6. Delegation of planning	1	2	3	
7. Aspirations to quality	1	2	3	
8. Infrastructure for member care and involvement	1	2	3	
9. Effective conflict prevention and management	1	2	3	
			Total Points	

B. Attendance for past 52 weeks beginning _____ (Date)

Gather attendance figures for each of the past 52 Sundays,* including Easter. (*Congregations with Saturday evening or Sunday evening alternatives to Sunday morning worship should include unduplicated attendance at these services in their weekly count.) If your primary Christmas service falls on a Sunday, eliminate that Sunday and count twice the attendance for the following Sunday. For each Sunday,* count the total number of people of any age who attended or who served as a leader in one or more of the following: sabbath worship services; church school for children, youth, or adults; nursery care during worship. Count each person only once for a given weekend. Total all 52 weeks and record in box below.

Grand Total for 52 Weeks

No divide this total by 52 and record in the box to the right. This is your 52-week average.

C. Plotting Your Location

Now use your System Change Index score (total points from part A), and your 52-week attendance average (from part B) to locate your congregation on the chart (figure 12). On the vertical axis, make a mark corresponding to your System Change Index score. On the horizontal axis, make a mark corresponding to your average attendance. As on any other graph, make a mark where the two ratings intersect. (The curved bands do not affect your plotting; they only affect your interpretation.)

Biblical Reflections

FIRST REFLECTION:
OUT IN THE WILDERNESS

Meditative Reading

The biblical books of Exodus and Numbers describe a period of discontinuous change in the life of the people of Israel. This discontinuity was precipitated, perhaps over a period of many years, by very bad news in the environment—the rise of a pharaoh who didn't remember Joseph's contribution to Egyptian life and so had no qualms about cruelty to the Hebrew slaves. He demanded more bricks and took away the supplies of straw the workers needed to make them.

This great period of discontinuity in Israel's life was more immediately precipitated by good news—God's call to Moses to confront Pharaoh and lead the people out of slavery. Their deliverance from slaughter and miraculous walk across the sea bed became the cornerstone of Israel's faith and ritual. But God's promise of a new pattern of life in a new land required that they first endure a period of chaos in the wilderness.

Despite the clear vision of God's purposes given to Moses, the people were frequently confused, frightened, and angry. The experience of slavery had been oppressive but predictable. Life in the wilderness, on the other hand, was terribly uncertain. Food and water were often in doubt, and they were crossing through the territory of alien peoples. Every new circumstance demanded of them a radical trust in God and a profound cooperation with their leaders.

Is God with us here, in these new circumstances? Is God powerful enough to care for us in today's unforgiving terrain? Do our leaders hear the voice of God, or only their own private dreams and desires? Do we, together, have a sufficient sense of God's call to maintain our communal bonds even as we pass through a wild frontier? These are the deep questions your congregation must struggle with in a time of size transition.

Group Bible Study

Exodus 15 describes the very beginning of the wilderness experience. In verse 21, we can still hear the tones of Miriam's song, celebrating God's mighty act of liberation. By the end of verse 22, the people have been without water for three days and are angry with Moses for bringing them out into this unknown and insecure place.

1. Read Exodus 15:20-27, and note your first reactions. Have you ever been in danger of real physical harm from a lack of water, perhaps on a camping trip? If not, what do you imagine it is like to fear you may die of thirst?
2. What thoughts and feelings might Moses have had in this first stage of the journey? What is it like to have your leadership questioned?
3. What wilderness periods has your congregation experienced in the past? Listen to the details of these stories, and see if you can find a pattern in the way your church handles such experiences.
4. If you have identified that your church is in a size transition, can you name aspects that feel like wilderness? Can you think of any gifts that God has given to sustain you in this wilderness journey?

SECOND REFLECTION:
OBSESSED WITH NUMBERS?

Meditative Reading

Should we be so concerned about numbers? I want to turn again to the account of the wilderness experience, most of which is recorded in the part of the scriptures called Numbers by Christians. The Hebrew title for this book refers to the journey in the wilderness, but it acquired an alternate title because the very first task on the wilderness journey was a census.

Does that seem strange? There they were in the wild borderland between their old life as slaves in Egypt and their new life in a land of promise. Was God's call to them simply about numbers? Of course not. But the people needed to know where they stood in this time of transition, and leaders needed to assess what the journey would require. So they counted.

Numbers do not determine our vocation as congregations. As persons and as faith communities, we listen for and respond to the voice of a living God. But one way to prepare for that sacred conversation about vocation is to look carefully—with an attitude of contemplation—at the numerical facts. This requires courage. We may be afraid that the picture will depress us or cause us to be blamed for the congregation's anxieties about growth. We may be afraid that the picture will challenge us to relinquish things we hold dear. Will God be with us then? Will the pillar of cloud by day and the pillar of fire by night still go ahead of us to guide our journey? Faith says yes, even as fear says no.

Group Bible Study

The opening chapters of the book of Numbers contain Israel's "marching orders" for the journey in the wilderness, beginning with a careful census of each tribe. Clearly, this is seen as essential preparation for the 40 transitional years ahead.

1. Why do you think that a census was important?
2. How do you feel about the act of recording and counting attendance or membership?
3. How can numbers be misused?
4. Besides attendance trends, what other numerical information might be helpful to our congregation as we seek to discern our calling today?

Third Reflection:
The Smell of Onions

Meditative Reading

A classic prayer asks for the grace to love and serve God "with gladness and singleness of heart." Both joy and single-mindedness start to run short in a size transition; they are replaced by profound ambivalence. Once a church has entered the plateau zone, the strength and appeal of the previous size is already compromised, while the virtues of the next size are not yet in place. Leaders find themselves in a "lose-lose" position because two competing sets of expectations are laid upon them. Confusion, anxiety, and indecision often result.

Some of the most poignant passages in Exodus and Numbers describe the ambivalence of the faith community in its transition from the land of bondage to the land of promise. When the people first left Egypt, they were so daunted by their transitional circumstances that some of them wished aloud: "If only we had died by the hand of the Lord in the land of Egypt, when we sat by the fleshpots and ate our fill of bread" (Exod. 16:3).

Once they had received the Law and moved on from Sinai, they even began to remember Egypt as a place flowing with milk and honey—a description usually reserved for the promised land. Their attention constantly drifted from God's mighty acts to the most domestic of details. "We remember the fish we used to eat in Egypt for nothing, the cucumbers, the melons, the leeks, the onions, and the garlic; but now our strength is dried up, and there is nothing at all but this manna to look at." (Num. 11:5-6).

Group Bible Study

1. Read Numbers 11:4-9. Why do you think this passage talks about food in such detail?
2. Can you imagine yourself wanting to go back to Egypt? Why or why not?
3. As your church considers issues of size transition, what do you already miss that might be comparable to the Israelites' longing for savory smells from their kitchens in Egypt?
4. If your congregation moved solidly into program size, what do you imagine to be the greatest loss you personally would have to deal with?

FOURTH REFLECTION:
WAITING FOR CLARITY

Meditative Reading

The people of Israel never went forward in the wilderness as long as the way was clouded. Until God provided a clear direction, they waited and watched and prayed.

Group Bible Study

1. Read Numbers 9:15-23. Why do you think that passage is so repetitive?
2. Can you identify a time in your own life when clarity was slow in coming? What helped you stick to the process of discernment until a direction became clear?
3. Outline the particular steps your congregation has gone through so far as it seeks to discern the desire of God about changing size? What missing steps may be clouding your decision?

FIFTH REFLECTION:
IS DIFFERENCE THE SAME AS DIVISION?

Meditative Reading

In Numbers 11, we see an example of the faith community wanting to enforce uniformity of religious experience. Eldad and Medad are not with the 70 elders gathered around the tent of meeting (their official place of communion with God); instead, they are having a profound encounter with the Spirit back in the camp.

Group Bible Study

1. Read Numbers 11:24-30. Why do you think Joshua wanted Moses to stop Eldad and Medad from expressing the Spirit of God in the camp?
2. What new demands does a congregation experience when everyone does not gather at the same hour for worship?
3. What greater richness of religious expression might be possible for your church if you had an additional sabbath service?
4. Can an additional service create a bridge with some groups of people in our community that God is trying to reach?

Sixth Reflection:
Learning to Delegate

Meditative Reading

Soon after the people of Israel had left Egypt, Moses encountered a personal crisis: he had slipped into the assumption that he personally had to solve all problems and fill all needs. It seems that Moses' family could see more clearly than he could what this style of ministry was doing to him. Jethro took him aside and suggested that he experiment with a different way to use his gifts and to organize for ministry.

Group Bible Study

1. Read Exodus 18:13-23. Imagine that Zipporah (the wife of Moses) has been speaking to her father, Jethro, just before the passage begins. What complaints might Zipporah have expressed to her father?
2. Would it have been easy for you to accept Jethro's advice? What prevents you from delegating parts of a task to other leaders?
3. Can you identify some specific ministries in your church which are unnecessarily burdensome because they now fall on just one person, or on just a few?
4. What advice do you imagine Jethro might have for your congregation regarding its staffing pattern or its way of organizing its ministries?

REFLECTION SEVEN:
PORTABLE TREASURES OF FAITH

Meditative Reading

When the people of Israel left Sinai to begin their 40 years of transition, they did not go alone. God showed them a way to take the "holy ground" of Sinai with them wherever they went. The ark of the covenant became the receptacle for their "portable treasures of faith."

In this exercise you will assemble the portable treasures that symbolize for your congregation the promise of God's presence, no matter where the journey may take you. This may be done by the learning team, by team and board together, or by the wider circle of leaders.

Group Bible Study

1.   Read Exodus 25:10-22. Bring into the room a large, decorated cardboard box to symbolize the ark.
2.   Identify the "portable treasures of faith" your congregation has been given by God—the beliefs, practices, and values that you can carry with you into any future and still express your deepest identity as God's people. Give people craft supplies and ask each to create a symbol of one "portable treasure" that seems absolutely essential for the journey ahead.
3.   In a period of worship, ask each person to describe their symbol, thank God for the gift it represents, and place it in the ark. Appoint one or two scribes for this ceremony who will write down what each person says about their symbol. Create a special place where the box will remain during the time the congregation is discerning God's call with respect to size and creating a plan for action. Go back to the symbols as often as you need to in order to stay in touch with what is truly essential.

Trend Scan:
The View from Here

As part of a general review and assessment process, AI asked its staff, consultants, and a variety of outside commentators to describe "the view from here." We asked them to cite the societal trends that they see affecting local congregations. Identifying those trends will help us to choose our future paths. We also hope the process will help congregations to locate themselves among the trends and to determine new courses of action.

Just as it is impossible to say exactly when a trend begins or ends, it is difficult to say exactly "where" any trend is or is moving at a given instant. So a project like this remains a work in progresss—loose, flexible, and liable to change. Nevertheless, we all need at certain points to try to "capture" a moment in time, to take a quick snapshot before the scene changes again. What follows is a list of elements that make up "the view from here" early in 1997.

SOCIOCULTURAL TRENDS

The U.S. is moving through a period of profound change characterized by increasing social, ethnic, cultural, and religious pluralism. Individuals and groups face unprecedented and overwhelming choices and strains in patterns of living and unprecedented diversity in the people and factors shaping the context for choice. At the dawn of the 21st century, the nation has no predominant value system or model of social life with which to confront the epic changes underway. Instead, it has a variety of models that are both stimulating in their breadth and confusing in their multiplicity. These models are often in conflict with one another.

At the same time as there is no generally accepted value system, there is no widely acknowledged authority positioned to influence or advocate today's values definitively. This reflects another major factor distinguishing our period of change: a lack of trust in authority generally and a particular disenchantment with groups formerly regarded as authoritative. These include government, politicians and the political process, civic leaders, educational institutions, law enforcement, the justice system, and institutional religion.

❏ **New diversity in the population**
Demographically, the U.S. is becoming ever more multiracial and multicultural, with new waves of immigration deepening our nation's experience of diversity. Census data show that the percentage of the population that is **foreign-born** has almost doubled since 1970 to 8.8%; it is now at its highest level since prior to World War II. Recent increases in ethnic diversity have produced centers of new energy and vitality (including religious vitality) where, for example, Hispanics, Asians, Indians, and people from eastern Europe have recently settled, reshaping cities such as Los Angeles, New York, Minneapolis, and Chicago.

There is more diversity in behavior and lifestyle as well as in ethnic origin. The proportion of U.S. households with married couples fell by 10% in the past 25 years to 78%. Gay and lesbian households have increased. The percentage of children living with two parents went from 85% in 1970 to 73% in 1994. Primarily because of economic factors, new household groups are also increasing, composed of intergenerational or nonrelated members.

While the population is further diversifying, it is also aging. The median age in the U.S. is 34.5 years—the oldest it has ever been. Between 1960 and 1994, the total U.S. population grew by 45%, but the population 65 years and older grew by 100%. Currently, 13% of the population is 65 or older. Many seniors live alone for increasingly longer periods of time.

❏ **Separation of age-groups**. The growing aging group contrasts with the 26% of the population who are under 18. Young and old are sometimes described as competing for the same scarce resources. They are also separated by communicating in different "languages." Earlier generations grew up on words; younger generations—raised on TV and computers—respond more strongly to images—an entirely different "language." The future world will be an electronic one in which communication will be based primarily on images.

U.S. Foreign Born Population, 1995

**Highest-Ranking
Countries of Birth of U.S.
Foreign-Born Population,
1995**

Country	Number in thousands
Mexico	6,719
Philippines	1,200
China/Taiwan/ Hong Kong	816
Cuba	797
Canada	695
El Salvador	650
Great Britain	617
Germany	598
Poland	538
Jamaica	531
Dominican Republic	509

| 1900 | 1910 | 1920 | 1930 | 1940 | 1950 | 1960 | 1970 | 1980 | 1990 | 1995 |

Source: Bureau of the Census, U.S. Dept. of Commerce

❑ There are **gains in racial equality and economic well-being** of African-Americans, but also **new or resurgent forms of racism** (Black church burnings) as well as attitudinal reversals on such issues as affirmative action. Hate groups have proliferated and are using technology to spread their message to more people.

❑ **Gender and sexuality issues** still figure prominently in public and church discussion. Since 1980, the percentage of women working outside the home has increased by 13%; 59% of all women over the age of 16 are in the labor force. Yet women still experience salary discrepancies with men, as well as "glass ceilings" in their efforts toward leadership advancement. **Abortion and homosexuality** influence political races and continue to affect public and church discussion. There are increasing reports of **sexual abuse** of children and sexual harassment of women. This has been a problem within churches as well as in the wider society.

❑ **Increasing globalization/increasing localism**
The U.S. is linked inextricably to the rest of the globe: the **global village** continues to shrink, due especially to technology. Political, economic, social, cultural, and religious forces increasingly operate across national and international boundaries. The same trends affecting North America–increased immigration and diversity–characterize other areas as well, particularly Europe. Recent epic changes such as the demise of communism and the economic rise of Asia directly affect life in the U.S.

While North Americans join international internet communities, they also tend to focus more on certain local realities than on the "big picture." This is due partly to mistrust of larger authorities. The very growth in power of global forces sometimes strengthens nationalism and local loyalties. Localism can be both reactionary parochialism and a sign of vital life.

❑ **A possible move away from individualism, toward community.**
Some commentators say that the "self-indulgence" of the 1960s-1980s is on the wane, with more interest being expressed in relationships and groups–as well as in political agendas that include a common good. Other pundits continue to argue that radical individualism is "the" American trait, especially regarding economic realities. People desire community, but seek it in new ways. Many interest or associational groups never meet in person, but connect over the internet, for example, allowing people to create new kinds of relationships. At the same time, there has been a notable reduction in domestic civic participation. Americans join fewer groups (they go "bowling alone" in the words of political scientist Robert Putnam), participate less in civic life, and vote less than they once did.

❑ In recent decades, Americans have felt they are living in an **"uncivil society."** There is a widespread perception that human relationships–personal, professional, in business and civic life–are coarsening. Indexers at Fordham University determined that the nation's sense of social well-being has fallen to its lowest point in almost 25 years. Many of people's actions are motivated by fear. From 1974 to 1993 violent crimes, including dramatic acts of terrorism, increased 63%. Domestic violence is also widely prevalent (and widely reported), as is the teenage suicide rate, which is

95% higher than it was in 1970. On the other hand, in the past year crime has gone down. Some fears are due simply to **perception**–often based on media images. For example, New York has a lower crime rate than Minneapolis, but nevertheless exemplifies urban evil to many Americans.

ECONOMIC TRENDS

❑   **The market economy dominates.** The American economy is globalizing rapidly. Analysts are divided on whether the global market will produce an era of peaceful prosperity or an eventual crash. The U.S. labor force feels its rights to fair wages have eroded; it blames both foreign workers and American management. White-collar and professional workers no longer have confidence in job security. Meanwhile, the economy is growing (a gain not reflected equally in every part of society), and many people feel more well-off than they did ten years ago.

Areas once regarded as civic (or sometimes religious) responsibilities–education, the dispensation of justice, civic improvement–have become regarded as **commodities**, subject to market rules and descriptions. Rich school districts offer much better education than do poor school districts; in some cases, public schools have actually been taken over and run by private corporations as profit-making enterprises. "How much justice can you afford?" is a phrase heard increasingly as perceptions deepen that the court system is biased against the poor.

In the U.S., the gap between rich and poor continues to grow. It is currently greater than at any time since the end of World War II –by some estimates since the 1920s. Between 1983 and 1989, the top 20% of wealth holders received 99% of the total gain in marketable wealth. Census data show that the top 20% hold almost 47% of the nation's wealth; the next 20% hold around 23%. The lowest 60% hold about 30%. The mean income for the top 20% in 1994 was $91,000 (for the top 5% it was almost $141,000); for the lowest 20% it was a little below $8,000. The Fordham study concluded that in the mid-1990s, the gap worsened more quickly than any other problem except food stamp coverage. Access of the privileged to expensive technology (in medicine and communication, for example) increases the gap between rich and poor.

Religion, too, is subject to market impact, as churches struggle to dispense fair wages and benefits, buy or construct buildings, pay legal costs, balance domestic and international needs, and take on increasing social service responsibilities. Religion is perceived in market terms: it is a commodity for which people "shop" and to which they feel a commitment only as long as it "serves their needs." Religious groups use market techniques to communicate their message.

EDUCATION AND TRAINING

❑ **Technological change has made education an elitist commodity.** The pervasive dominance of computers and technology has contributed to making education uneven and unequal. Job success today usually requires some knowledge of computers, but many poor school districts (let alone individuals) are still without them. In 1993, 35.8% of white youth had access to a computer, while only 13% of black youth and 12% of Hispanic youth did. Those left behind in the race for techno-skills must compete with unskilled labor around the world for low wages.

On the other hand, more high school graduates are going to college. And more people are graduating from college than in the past.

SCIENCE AND TECHNOLOGY

❑ **More data, less wisdom?** There is a proliferation of far more data than the society at large can process or understand. But turning data into wisdom remains an ongoing challenge. Science retains an aura of mystery, and we rely on its experts (although the use of obscure and anti-rational thought is also common). On the other hand, as basic technological knowledge spreads, so do dangers ranging from homemade bombs to the capability to invade government, business, and personal computers.

Increasing numbers of people recognize a need to protect the earth. In last fall's elections, environmental legislation in states generally passed. The government may challenge industry and commerce toward tighter controls. There are new partnerships working to improve the situation; for example, the Union of Concerned Scientists is producing educational materials in cooperation with the National Religious Partnership for the Environment.

At the same time, there is still much confusion about "scientific proof" for many basic problems. For example, one position states that smoking definitely causes cancer, while another position says there is no scientific proof of cause and effect. On the global front, **population explosion** continues to strain natural resources. But some people do not consider population growth an addressable "environmental" issue like recycling or industrial pollution, especially when its effects seem so far away.

A number of new books bring **science and religion closer together**, as scientists find religious ideas increasingly compatible with the scientific discoveries about the origins of the universe. People look to science for help with ethical issues such as artificial life-support, genetic engineering, or defining the moment of death.

RELIGIOUS REALITIES

American society displays a strong interest in religion, and many commentators have written of widespread spiritual hunger. People still look to religion for **meaning and values**. However, many of them look less to religion for **authority** than they once did. Seekers seem more interested in spirituality than in religion, especially institutional religion, and most especially, mainline religion. But other people seek strong authority in organized religion: around the world, all major faiths have seen the rise of fundamentalisms. In the U.S., most fundamentalist and evangelical churches have grown or maintained membership.

Changes in attitudes about authority and leadership coincide with changes in how information is disseminated and how people want it to be disseminated—both within the church and in the wider world. During the age of Christian/Protestant dominance, means of communication and authority suggested a solid image like a building—perhaps like the Athenian Parthenon. An overall roof of Christian values, ideas, and goals was supported by numerous vertical columns, each representing a denomination or communion. Information and authority flowed vertically form the roof down the columns, while each column remained separate and distinct as well, containing its own particular ethos and identity.

The situation is different today. Instead of an image of a building, another type of image—such as a web—may be more appropriate. In a web there is not just one way to receive information, ideas, or leadership. Rather, parts of the web are connected in various ways that allow communication to move horizontally, vertically, diagonally, or in various paths.

These general changes in ways of describing communication and social interaction underlie all of the many other ways in which parts of the religious world are changing.

❑ **Congregations are changing.**

Membership in the mainline is **aging**. It has also generally been losing members for some time. Participation and financial support have also been declining. Mainline congregations need to serve both long-time members and newer, younger members, who have **different expectations**. As a result of these pressures, some congregations are engaging in experiments with new models of ministry, such as mega-churches, "alternative" services, evening services, and so on. Other congregations are attempting to hold fast to earlier models.

Parishioners express a desire for a more intense feeling of **community**, yet they have difficulty defining or finding exactly what they mean. Small groups have been a major effort to address this need in congregations.

Teen-agers and young adults seem disconnected from mainline congregational life. There have now been several generations of biblically illiterate youth, and even those within the churches are not necessarily trained in the basics of the faith or the denomination. Major efforts to revamp youth programs are underway.

Some observers see an increasing sense of tension and **conflict** between clergy and laity. This may arise around **financial issues**, issues of **authority**, or other matters. When problems do occur, they often seem a result of confusion and lack of understanding. For example, in the financial area, laity and clergy may not have the same understanding of the financial resources a pastor needs. Because new leadership models are emerging for both clergy and laity, it may be unclear who has **authority** to make a particular decision or organize a congregational ministry program.

Finances are a huge concern for congregations—with some falling below the minimum level to continue operations. Yet there are also creative new movements such as coalitions, church-to-church loan programs, or organizations of endowed churches seeking cooperation and mutual advice to address the economic needs of their own and other congregations.

Congregations are undoubtedly here to stay. As religious people continue to focus locally, the local church will remain primary. However, congregations may dramatically change shape. They may merge into denominational clusters, become ecumenical congregations, hire several part-time clergy, increase lay ministry, offer radically new types of services, or repro-gram their ministries to reflect the aging of their members. Observers such as sociologist of religion Nancy Ammerman argue that perhaps more than anything else, congregations are shaped by—and must take account of—member **transience and movement**.

❑ **Denominations have shrunk**. Mainline denominations struggle with issues of diversity and identity. Signs of major change have abounded: mem-bership loss, downsizing, restructuring, decline in financial well-being.

Members of local congregations have only a vague notion of what a denominational headquarters does. Denominational leaders are buffeted by criticism from every direction. Many are searching for new understanding of what it means to be a denomination in late-modern America. Some would interpret these trends as a breakdown; others as an indication that religious faith may be moving out of a bureaucratic age back to its roots in small, local groups.

Denominational identity is not a major concern of many congrega-tions. Denominational barriers are increasingly permeable, with church choice for many people based on factors like location or style rather than denomi-nation. Many local congregations seem to practice a sort of natural ecumenism. Some analysts would say that this is not a "real" **ecumenism** because it has not developed out of deep theological conversations; others, taking a more experiential approach, affirm the validity of this sort of ecumenism. Congregations wishing to be ecumenical are searching for re-sources.

Interest groups and networks exist across denominations. These often form around social, political, or personal-lifestyle issues. Examples include the "green movement," groups focusing on women's issues, and groups based on sexual affinity or attitudes toward abortion.

Bilateral and more broadly based talks between and among denomina-tions are bringing them closer together. There has been **interfaith coop-eration** on such concerns as the environment and aid for refugees.

The role of **middle judicatories** is evolving. Decline in finances and increase in local congregational focus are giving rise to redefinition of judi-catory roles. Leaders are experiencing a loss of morale as they deal with cutbacks in resources and increased competition among resource provid-ers. But there is also energetic experimentation going forward to revision judicatory roles, for example, moving away from programmatic focus to other supporting and coordinating activitities.

❑   **Clergy roles are evolving.**

The **place of clergy** in the society and in the congregation continues to change. In addition to role confusion, there is the general loss of esteem that has affected many former authority figures. Yet many older or second-career people feel called to ministry, to which they bring gifts of experience and wisdom. In general, clergy leadership in the mainline mirrors the aging of its laity. If the enrollment of older persons in seminary is not balanced with an increase in younger seminarians, the mainline will have problems in future years with inadequate numbers of clergy.

The entry of **women** into ministry is changing its face forever. In 1972, 10% of seminarians were women; in 1993, 31%. Women have brought creative new leadership styles to the church. Yet they still occupy few top positions in "tall steeple" churches or in denominations.

Seminary education is also changing. Theological schools are beginning to require a pre-entry level of basic church knowledge, are expanding programs such as off-site learning, and are introducing new recruitment plans to attract younger students. They are also making spirituality a more central part of the educational experience, a focus encouraged in new accreditation standards adopted by the Association of Theological Schools. Some seminaries are working more in groups or clusters to avoid duplication of offerings and resources.

❑   **Laity are searching.**

Laypeople, especially women, says sociologist of religion Wade Clark Roof, are filling new leadership roles and introducing new concerns, such as holistic health and increased integration of faith and life, into congregational awareness. There is confusion as new styles of leadership develop. Both clergy and laity need resources to help them define their respective roles.

Laity are searching for connections to other types of resources they want, especially in areas of spirituality. They often turn to "new religions" while unaware that resources exist within their own faith tradition.

Conclusion

It is appropriate to end this scan with a reference to searching. We are all searching, really. What we find depends on how we search. The U.S., along with the rest of the world, stands not only on the brink of a new century, but on the brink of an era during which reshaping of identities will predominate. The many seemingly contradictory movements and trends cited here suggest the many alternatives for that reshaping process.

People do not want pat solutions; they want to find answers in creative combinations. More choice is required—but more options are available. This transitional time offers a unique opportunity for close re-examination of mission—what we might call "mission in movement." This is as true for the Alban Institute as it is for the congregations, groups, organizations, judicatories, and denominations that it serves.

Reprinted by permission from CONGREGATIONS: *The Alban Journal*, published by the Alban Institute, Inc., 7315 Wisconsin Avenue, Suite 1250W, Bethesda, MD 20814-3211. Copyright © 1997. All rights reserved.

"Snapshot" Page from a Percept "Ministry Area Profile"

"Snapshot" Page from a Percept "Ministry Area Profile"

Snapshot

Prepared For:
Massachusetts Conference UCC
ImagineArea #4
W. Cambridge, MA

Study Area Definition:
3.0 Mile Radius

Coordinates: 42:23:02 71:11:79
Date: 6/11/99

Primary U.S. Lifestyles Segments—1999

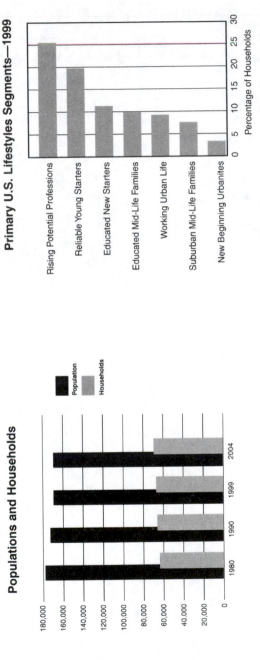

Populations and Households

The population in the study area has decreased by 4142 persons or 2.4% since 1990 and is projected to increase by 41 persons, or 0.0% between 1999 and 2004. The number of households has increased by 1009, or 1.5% since 1990 and is projected to increase by 1662, or 2.4% between 1999 and 2004.

Population By Race/Ethnicity—1999

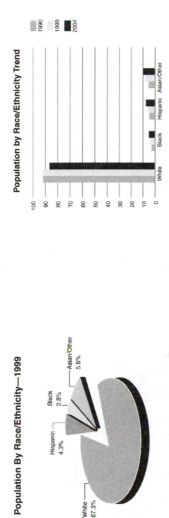

White 87.3%

Hispanic 4.3%

Black 2.8%

Asian/Other 5.6%

Population by Race/Ethnicity Trend

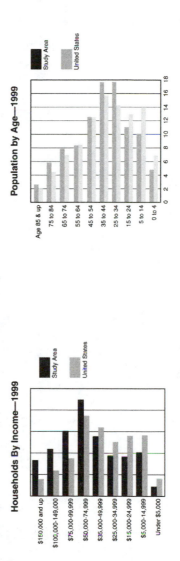

Between 1999 and 2004, the White population is projected to decrease by 4252 persons and to decrease from 87.3% to 84.7% of the total population. The Black population is projected to increase by 850 persons and to increase from 2.8% to 3.3% of the total. The Hispanic/Latino population is projected to increase by 1151 persons and to increase from 4.3% to 4.9% of the total. The Asian/Other population is projected to increase by 2292 persons and to increase from 5.6% to 7.0% of the total population

Households By Income—1999

Population by Age—1999

The average household income in the study area is $69965 a year compared to the U.S. average of $53198. The average age in the study area is 39.9 and is projected to increase to 40.8 by 2004. The average age in the U.S. is 36.5 and is projected to increase to 37.3 by 2004.

(800) 442-5277

© 1998-99 Percept Group, Inc.

Sources: Percept, National Decision Systems, U.S. Census Bureau

ID# 20338:6-543

Should We Add a New Worship Service?

A Key Decision

If you believe that moving through a size transition is the faithful thing to do, you will need to look at the number and type of worship opportunities you are providing. Based on his research with North American Protestant churches, church growth specialist Charles Arn has concluded that about half our congregations are good candidates for adding a new worship opportunity of a somewhat different style: "Of churches that do begin a new service, eight out of ten will experience a *measurable increase* in 1) total worship attendance, 2) total giving, and 3) number of Christian conversions."[1]

Which half of the congregations are good candidates? Arn says it is easier to describe the situations in which adding a service is *not* a good bet. Don't try to add a service if the church's top priority is "community" (bringing everyone together at the same time for weekly worship), correct theology, or survival. And don't try to do it when the primary pastor is planning to leave in the next year or so. In the great majority of other churches, adding a service will foster overall growth.

Many of the assumptions that discourage church leaders from trying a new service were found to be invalid. For example, it is not true that small churches can't add worship opportunities—a church with an attendance of 40 or more is big enough to start a second service. Nor is it true that only growing churches should add a worship service; indeed, decline is an even stronger signal to try something new.

Further, leaders often assume that they should only start an additional service when the sanctuary is full.[2] Arn found some interesting, counter-intuitive relationships between seating capacity and the success of a new worship opportunity. When the church is less than 40 percent full, a new service is *especially* appropriate because the current service is unlikely to grow and unlikely to be impacted negatively by the new one. Adding a service is a touchier matter in a church whose attendance has remained plateaued for several years at 60 to 80 percent of seating capacity, because the new service under those conditions may well draw off some of the current service's strength. Even so, says Arn, starting a new worship opportunity still creates the greatest likelihood of an overall increase in attendance. If a church is actually filled up already (80 to 100 percent of capacity), he recommends the immediate creation of an *identical* service, rather than one of a somewhat different style.

WHY TRY SOMETHING DIFFERENT?

Arn has identified several strong reasons for expanding the worship opportunities and the range of worship styles. First on the list is the impact on those who are not currently worshipping anywhere. The creation of a new service helps a congregation focus its attention on those who are not here yet, and it challenges leaders to convey the core message in fresh ways. The new service makes it easier for people to invite friends and neighbors. This last point is worth emphasizing. People often hesitate to invite because they don't have confidence that their church's familiar patterns will connect with others; when a meaningful new opportunity is planned, the number of invitations increases dramatically.

The increased variety of times and styles will also minister better to the range of people who are already on our church rolls—active and inactive. The broader culture today fosters in people the expectation that they will have choices in their religious involvement right along with other aspects of their lives. Offering another major worship opportunity, at a different time and in a somewhat different style, guarantees that more kinds of people can participate in our church life without disrupting the patterns that have proven meaningful for many current members. A blended approach (older and newer elements in the same service) often ends up frustrating everyone and undermining the financial stability of the congregation in the process.

WHAT IS A "SOMEWHAT DIFFERENT" STYLE?

One of Arn's most helpful contributions to the conversation about multiple worship services is his diagram of the different population groups a given service might be addressing. He incorporates three variables into his scheme. First, he speaks of three generational groupings: seniors (born before 1940), baby boomers (those now arriving at middle age), and the baby bust generation (born after 1965). Second, in relation to faith participation, he distinguishes between believers and seekers. And on the third dimension of social and ethnic identity, he conceives that worship can be oriented toward people of the same culture, people of multiple cultures, or people of a different culture than the dominant group in the congregation. These different possibilities are represented in chart form:

Different Ways Worship Services Can Be Focused

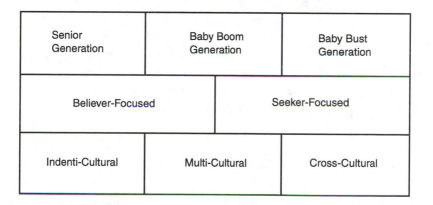

Theoretically, there are 18 unique approaches to worship that could be fashioned by choosing one emphasis from each row. But current church life is not nearly that diverse. Arn found that an astounding 96 percent of existing services are designed for people closer to the left-hand side of the chart—believers from the senior or boomer generations who share the same cultural background as existing members. Whether you intend it or not, your church's worship is currently shaped to meet the needs and expectations of some groups more than others.

To plan a new service which will increase your church's total attendance, Arn recommends that you move to *one* adjacent box on only *one* row. One change in one variable will be significant enough to attract an entirely new group of people. Changing more than one variable will make the process of researching and planning the new service not just twice as complicated, but four times so. Changing all three variables to define a new service will require a Herculean effort and reduce the chances of success dramatically.[3]

So, the 96 percent of churches on the left side of the chart will set themselves up for failure if they try, in one jump, to reach non-believer young adults of a different socioeconomic group. Instead, each church can ponder its vocation and gifts (in relation to the community context) and determine just one dimension of learning and change that it will attempt in the next few years. Believer seniors may decide to reach out to seeker seniors instead of looking for young families. A multi-cultural congregation of boomers may focus only on providing a worship option for culturally similar neighbors and offspring in their early twenties.

There is an appealing modesty in this approach. Once we get over the illusion that our church is actually reaching everybody, we can take one clear step toward becoming more inclusive. The modest one-box move is still a demanding goal, requiring deep commitment and perseverance on the part of leaders and members. A church that succeeds in serving one additional subgroup in the population through a sustainable new worship service is much more likely, I believe, to take additional missionary risks in the future.

A Look at the Costs

In order to explore the promising possibility of an additional service, clergy and elected leaders will have to confront their own significant fears, as well as those of the current members. One denomination[4] discovered that pastors and boards were apprehensive about many of the same things, including:

- Physical demands on the clergy
- Loss of unity due to separate congregations; not knowing everyone
- Psychological let-down due to diminishment of the existing service
- Conflict, decreased morale, or a drop in overall attendance

In addition to these common themes, the clergy had substantial fears about the failure of the new project (lack of cooperation or low attendance), while boards were anxious about trying something new and different. The news was good, however, from congregations that actually implemented a new service; respondents to the study all reported that their churches "now felt positive toward the new service, and that it was worth the time, money, and risk involved."[5]

Although those positive results are encouraging, we shouldn't assume that the risk ends when the new service begins to succeed. Pastors will be subject to criticism whether the new service succeeds or not. Arn found that there are three periods when the risk to the pastor peaks: (1) the period between first public airing of the idea and a formal vote; (2) the first three months of the new service; and (3) the 8- to 12- month period after attendance at the new service exceeds attendance at previously existing services.

The first two periods of high risk seem predictable enough, but the third may take leaders by surprise. What we see there is the risk of success:

> In churches that have had only one service or style for ten years or more, the success of the new service may cause greater consternation among many members than would its failure. If the service is successful, the pastor's risk is in the reaction from those who have sanctified the status quo.[6]

Clergy will be ill-equipped to face this kind of risk without a healthy network of emotional support. They will need spiritual guidance from a reliable person or group outside their work setting (which includes both the congregation and the denominational hierarchy) and even some perspective on how they would support themselves financially if they were to leave this particular position.[7]

Arn found that clergy tenure is also a significant factor in determining the costliness of this initiative. During the first year or two, a pastor may succeed in launching a new service as his or her first major project because of the "honeymoon" phenomenon. (The family-size church may be an exception here.) In the third through fifth years, the willingness of the congregation to follow a pastor's change initiative drops drastically, so that success will probably require "extraordinary support among established lay leaders," assurance of the pastor's commitment to stay long enough to get the service established, and a few respected leaders who will stand with the pastor when the going gets tough. Once a pastor enters the sixth year and intends to stay a while, members become more and more likely to accept change initiatives.

Pastors need to be prepared for an increased work load, not just to implement the additional service, but also to plan for it week by week and to organize the additional volunteer ministries that will support it. If the vision for the service involves reaching out with a moderately different style to an additional population, Arn suggests that the new service may require four times as much planning time as the current one—placing most of the attention not on development of a different sermon, but on preparation for the whole worship experience with a team of leaders, mostly gifted volunteers.

Critical Mass

The worst way to launch a new worship service is to start small and hope it will grow. It is perfectly normal for a new service to decline 20 to 50 percent during the first few months after it is inaugurated, and you should plan to start big enough to ensure that attendance does not drop below "critical mass" at any time during that period. Arn provides criteria for determining critical mass:

> *Attendance Goal #1*: At least 50 people or 35% of the largest present service (whichever is greater) in attendance. . . . Most new services that begin with less than 50 don't survive the first year. . . .
>
> *Attendance Goal #2*: At least 35% of those in attendance should be unchurched. . . .Churches generally find that if their new service is focused on a new target group, and adequate promotion to the target audience has occurred, then 65% or more of those in attendance will be unchurched or inactives. . .
>
> *Room Capacity Goal*: The meeting room should be filled to at least 50% capacity. . . . It may be better to meet in a facility other than the sanctuary.[8]

Critical mass is the "number of people needed to allow the service to continue to grow beyond the first six months." If a new service "begins below, or drops below, the critical mass in the first six months, there is often insufficient energy to begin growing again, and the service will probably die."[9]

Arn's research makes it clear that starting a new service is a challenge. But it is reassuring to know that a well-planned expansion of worship opportunities can help move a stuck congregation off an attendance plateau and even reverse the trend in a declining church.

APPLICATION EXERCISE

1. Prepare a seating chart for your church showing the number of people that can be accommodated comfortably (30 to 36 inches of space per person).

2. Prepare a parking chart showing how many cars can be accommodated at your main worship service. Ten minutes before each service starts, how many convenient spaces are visible to a first-time visitor?

3. For each of your services, chart the following information. The final column refers to Charles Arn's categories on page 165.

	Average attendance	Percentage of seating capacity utilized	Who this service is designed to reach (age group, believers/ seekers, cultural group)
Service A			
Service B			
Service C			

4. Review the first section of this chapter. To what extent is your church a good candidate for adding a new worship opportunity?

5. Unless your main service is already 80 percent full, Arn recommends that you create a new service of a somewhat different style using the "one-box rule" to define the change. For whom might a new service be designed?

Introduction

1. Smaller congregations can be subdivided into "family size" (up to 50 in attendance) and "pastoral size" (51–150). See chapter 2 for further information about the different sizes.

2. See Ronald Heifetz, *Leadership Without Easy Answers* (Cambridge, Mass.: Belknap Press), 36–40.

3. Ibid., 128.

Chapter 1

1. In this chapter, I am drawing together descriptions from several sources: my previous book, *The In-Between Church* (Bethesda, Md.: The Alban Institute, 1998); contributions by Dan Hotchkiss to the article, "Searching for the Key: Developing a Theory of Synagogue Size," *Congregations* 27, no. 1 (January–February 2001); a recent work by Gary McIntosh, *One Size Doesn't Fit All* (Grand Rapids: Revell, 1999); and some preliminary findings from the National Congregations Study (NCS) headed by Mark Chavez at the University of Arizona. "The tipping point" has become a household term because of Malcolm Gladwell's book, *The Tipping Point: How Little Things Can Make a Big Difference* (Boston: Little, Brown and Company, 2000).

2. British anthropologist Robin Dunbar, for example, has demonstrated a biological basis for the way primates organize themselves into groups. See R. I. M. Dunbar, "Neocortex size as a constraint on group size in primates," *Journal of Human Evolution* 20 (1992): 469–93. Cited from *The Tipping Point*, chapter 5.

3. *One Size Doesn't Fit All*, chapter 3. McIntosh's very simplified framework uses the figure 200 as the upper limit of the single-cell structure.

4. *Sizing Up a Congregation for New Member Ministry* (New York: Episcopal Church Center, Undated), 15. This resource was first distributed by the Episcopal Church in the mid-1980s.

5. Carl F. George, *How to Break Growth Barriers* (Grand Rapids: Baker Book House, 1993), 136. In this section George is quoting from Elmer Towns, *Ten of Today's Most Innovative Churches*, page 243.

6. This change is partly based on my observation that congregations rarely accomplish the full shift to a "program" identity and structure until attendance hit a critical mass of about 250. Gary McIntosh (*One Size Doesn't Fit All*) offers the figure 400 as the upper limit of "medium size."

7. Findings of the National Congregations Study (NCS) are based on a 1998 survey administered to a random sample of 1,236 congregations of all faiths. The study avoided the biases inherent in many previous studies of congregations by beginning with a representative sample of *persons*, then asking those persons if they were affiliated with a congregation. You can access this information on the web at www.alban.org/NCS.asp.

8. I have two reasons for making this equation. First, it has been my experience that "regular attendee" or "active member" estimates by leaders tend to be higher than the actual year-round averages. Second, even if the "regular attendee" figure were exactly equal to average sabbath attendance, I believe that these figures would still essentially describe a set of congregations that has moved fully into the "program" mode of operation. In my experience, this transition tends to be incomplete until the congregation is nearing the 250 mark. Further exploration of the NCS data set may yield more precise information over time.

9. Using the "regular attendee" measure of the NCS, about 94 percent of congregations have 499 or fewer.

10. Mark Chaves, *How Do We Worship?* (Bethesda, Md.: The Alban Institute, 1999), 8.

11. The two factors I have used to generate this finding are "number of regular attendees including children" (a figure estimated by the respondent) and "number of committees that have met in the past year." This and subsequent findings from the NCS data set reported in this chapter were derived using the "Create a Table" option on the NCS web site.

12. *One Size Doesn't Fit All*, chapter 3.

13. See n. 2, above.

Chapter 2

1. Alan C. Klaas and Cheryl D. Brown, *Church Membership Initiative: Research Summary of Findings* (Appleton, Wis.: Aid Association for Lutherans, 1993), 20–21.

2. Bill M. Sullivan, *Ten Steps to Breaking the 200 Barrie*r (Kansas City, Mo.: Beacon Hill Press, 1988), 51.

3. *The Alpha Course*, Cook Ministry Resources, www.AlphaNA.org; Disciple Bible Study, Cokesbury Press: 800-672-1789 (a special program requiring leader training by Cokesbury); *Disciples of Christ in Community*, Sewanee School of Theology Programs Center, 1-800-722-1974 (a special program requiring leader training by Sewanee).

4. Jean Morris Trumbauer, *Created and Called: Discovering Our Gifts for Abundant Living* (Minneapolis: Augsburg Fortress, 1998), 12.

5. Jean Morris Trumbauer, *Discovering the Gifts of the People* worksheets (Minneapolis: Augsburg Fortress, 1995). Can be purchased at minimal cost in a package of 50 worksheets, with one leader guide, from Augsburg Fortress (800-328-4648).

Chapter 3

1. Linda J. Clark, Joanne Swenson, and Mark Stamm, chapter 2 in *How We Seek God Together: Exploring Worship Style* (Bethesda, Md.: The Alban Institute, 2001). This book comes with a powerful video comparing the style (and therefore the culture) of three congregations.

2. David A. Roozen, William McKinney, and Jackson W. Carroll, *Varieties of Religious Presence, Mission in Public Life* (New York: Pilgrim Press, 1984), cited in *Handbook for Congregational Studies,* edited by Jackson W. Carroll, Carl S. Dudley, and William McKinney (Nashville: Abingdon Press, 1986), 29–30.

3. The "tool kit" metaphor comes from "Culture in Action: Symbols and Strategies," an article by sociologist Anne Swidler in *American Sociological Review* (April 1986). The article is cited in *How We Seek God Together* (see n. 1 above), chapter 2.

4. Nancy T. Ammerman, "Spiritual Journeys in the American Mainstream," *Congregations* 22, no. 1 (January–February 1997): 11–15.

5. The study included a group exploration of the congregation's history, plus individual interviews with the (full-time) pastors and two lay leaders in each church. The questions I asked in the individual interviews are found in appendix D.

6. Joanne Sabol Stevenson, "Construction of a Scale to Measure Load, Power and Margin in Life," *Nursing Research* 31, no. 4 (July–August 1982).

7. Celia Allison Hahn, *Growing in Authority, Relinquishing Control* (Bethesda, Md.: The Alban Institute, 1994), 28.

8. *Leader Behavior Analysis II* (Escondido, Calif: The Ken Blanchard Companies, 1999). A revised edition of this instrument is now available, called Situational Leadership II (SLII).

9. "Liberal" and "democratic" are relative terms. But even Protestant denominations with a hierarchical structure—Episcopal, Presbyterian, United Methodist, for example—still rely on elected governing boards and (on some issues) congregational meetings to authorize important changes.

10. This concept of the congregation as a "little public" comes from the work of the Religion in Urban America program of the University of Illinois at Chicago, which since 1992 has studied the experiences of some 75 congregations in the metropolitan area. Lowell W. Livezey directs the program. The Alban Institute will publish learnings from this work in 2002.

11. Charles Arn, "Multiple Worship Services and Church Growth," *Journal of the American Institute of Church Growth* 7 (1996): 96.

12. Denise W. Goodman, *Congregational Fitness: Healthy Practices for Layfolk* (Bethesda, Md.: The Alban Institute, 2000).

13. Gilbert R. Rendle, *Behavioral Covenants in Congregations: A Handbook for Honoring Differences* (Bethesda, Md.: The Alban Institute, 1999).

14. Gary L. McIntosh, *One Size Doesn't Fit All* (Grand Rapids: Fleming H. Revell, 1999), 46–48.

Chapter 4

1. Suzanne G. Farnham, Stephanie A. Hull, and R. Taylor McLean, *Grounded in God: Listening Hearts Discernment for Group Deliberations*, rev. ed. (Harrisburg, Penn.: Morehouse Publishing, 1999), 6. The book is available from online booksellers, as well as religious bookstores.

2. Major work on discernment practices in congregations is also being done by Charles M. Olsen and his colleagues at the Center for Transforming Religious Leadership (Worshipful-Work) in Kansas City, Mo. (816-891-1078). On the Internet at www.members.aol.com/worshpfulw/index.htm.

3. Available from The Alban Institute (800-486-1318). Segments 1a, 1b, 2a, and 2b would be especially helpful to learning team members—with a total viewing time of less than 40 minutes. Much of the same material is covered in my earlier book, *The In-Between Church* (Bethesda, Md.: The Alban Institute, 1998).

4. Based on the work of Gil Rendle for the Alban education event, "Strategic Planning in Congregations."

5. Jean Morris Trumbauer, *Discovering the Gifts of the People: Leader Guide* (Minneapolis: Augsburg Fortress, 1995): 1. She is citing O'Connor's work, *The Eighth Day of Creation* (Waco, Tex.: Word Books, 1971): 15.

6. Linda J. Clark, Joanne Swenson, and Mark Stamm, *How We Seek God Together: Exploring Worship Style* (Bethesda, Md.: The Alban Institute, 2001). This outstanding resource package is very inexpensive.

7. Celia Allison Hahn, *Uncovering Your Church's Hidden Spirit* (Bethesda, Md.: The Alban Institute, 2001).

8. Ibid, page 95.

9. Gil Rendle, *Living into the New World: How Cultural Trends Affect Your Congregation* (Bethesda, Md.: The Alban Institute, 2000).

10. Alan C. Klaas, *In Search of the Unchurched: Why People Don't Join Your Congregation* (Bethesda, Md.: The Alban Institute, 1996). At the end of chapter 10, Klaas provides a summary of these transitions and an exercise for discussion that would be very appropriate for your team, and perhaps for other groups in your congregation.

11. Percept Group, Inc., 151 Kalmus Drive, Suite A 104, Costa Mesa, CA 92626. 800-442-6277.

12. Gil Rendle, *Behavioral Covenants in Congregations: A Handbook for Honoring Differences* (Bethesda, Md.: The Alban Institute, 1999).

13. Denise W. Goodman, *Congregational Fitness: Healthy Practices for Layfolk* (Bethesda, Md.: The Alban Institute, 2000).

14. Katie Day, *Difficult Conversations: Taking Risks, Acting with Integrity* (Bethesda, Md.: The Alban Institute, 2001).

Appendix I

1. Charles, Arn. "Multiple Worship Services and Church Growth," *Journal of the American Society of Church Growth* 7 (1996): 73.

2. Ibid. Arn says that seating-capacity estimates must be updated with cultural change. A pew that was estimated to seat five people a generation ago would now comfortably seat only three because the comfort zone has grown to 30 to 36 inches.

3. Ibid., p 88.

4. Ibid., p. 94. Arn is citing a study by the Church of the Nazarene.

5. Ibid.

6. Ibid., p. 95.

7. See Roy Oswald's book *Clergy Self-Care: Finding a Balance for Effective Ministry* (Washington, D.C.: The Alban Institute, 1991).

8. Arn, "Multiple Worship Services and Church Growth," pp. 103-4.

9. Ibid., p. 101.